OH, COME ON ALL YE FAITHFUL!
A Humorous Church Collection

Heavenly anecdotes, deadly epitaphs, prize parish notices; from true stories from the Bishop's Palace to apocryphal tales from the rectory – these are just some of the offerings collected by Derek Nimmo in his lighthearted and affectionate anthology.

Famous men of the cloth like Bishops Wilberforce, Stubbs and Gore rub shoulders with lesser known parish priests, curates, churchwardens and laity as Derek Nimmo rummages through vestry and vicarage, cassock and chasuble, and the wider world beyond the lych-gate and yews, revealing that, in its humour at least, the Church of England is more than one former Dean of Salisbury's 'refrigerator van on the back of a train'.

About the author:

Derek Nimmo is an actor, producer and writer who must have played more Anglican clergymen than any other performer in history. He also numbers clerics of all kinds among his friends and acquaintances.

His many West End appearances include THE AMOROUS PRAWN, CHARLIE GIRL and SEE HOW THEY RUN. His many successful television situation comedies include LIFE BEGINS AT FORTY, THIRD TIME LUCKY and a string of popular programmes in which he's had to wear either a habit or a cassock, starting with ALL GAS AND GAITERS, followed by OH BROTHER! OH FATHER, and most recently HELL'S BELLS.

Oh, Come On All Ye Faithful!

A Humorous Church Collection

Derek Nimmo

CORONET BOOKS
Hodder and Stoughton

British Library C.I.P.
Nimmo, Derek
Oh, come on all ye faithful :
a humorous church collection.
1. Church of England
—— Anecdotes, facetiae, satire, etc.
2. English wit and humor
I. Title
828'.91407'08   PN6231.C3/

ISBN 0 340 41537 1

Printed and bound in Great Britain
for Hodder and Stoughton
Paperbacks, a division of Hodder and
Stoughton Ltd., Mill Road,
Dunton Green, Sevenoaks, Kent
TN13 2YA.
(Editorial Office: 47 Bedford Square,
London WC1B 3DP) by
Cox & Wyman Ltd., Reading

CONTENTS

Foreword

It is exactly twenty years ago since I was standing in my usual vague way, sipping a tiny tissue-restorer in the BBC Club at Shepherds Bush. Across the bar stood the newly appointed head of television comedy, one F. Muir, bow-tied and eyes a-twinkle. Something in my rather vacuous expression must have struck a tiny chord. 'Nimmo,' he said, sliding a crisp white script towards me along the bar, 'read this. The part's the Chaplain.' When I had taken the script home, I discovered it was for a pilot for the current comedy playhouse series about the inmates of a cathedral close.

The little play was *Behold a White Horse* and after it had been transmitted, and received tolerable acclaim, Frank commissioned from its authors – Edward Apse and Pauline Delaney – a series which he entitled *All Gas and Gaiters* from a quotation that he had somewhere excavated from Dickens's *Nicholas Nickleby*.

From thereon forward, my theatrical fate was sealed. Over the last two decades I seem to have wandered through an assortment of ecclesiastical parts, playing well-meaning, but slightly ineffectual clerics, starting with the Reverend Mervyn Noote and reaching at the moment of writing, by ill-merited promotion, Dean Selwyn Makepeace in my current series, *Hell's Bells*. As an ecumenical gesture, I played Brother Dominic in the *Oh Brother* series; after he had completed his novitiate, this became *Oh Father*. I still have the highest hopes of appearing in my old age as *Oh Pope!*

The non-conformist church I have somewhat

neglected, which must have brought considerable relief to assorted Baptists, Wesleyans, Episcopalians and even the occasional Jehovah's Witness. I have recently, however, received some rather splendid scripts for a Salvation Army comedy series from one of that movement's more masochistic captains. It seems a frightfully good idea – I rather fancy myself with a tambourine.

Of course, appearing so often as a clergyman has landed me in a deal of fairly hot water. I once made the mistake of saying, in a television interview, when asked what I felt about people making fun of the Church, that 'one should always be able to laugh at something that one loves'. I spent the next few weeks replying to indignant fellow Anglicans, explaining that because one has an affection for something, it is not necessarily a disrespect to find it amusing.

To the more belligerent letters, I sent a photocopy of St Paul's letter to the people of Corinth (I-13); that always has an extremely calming effect and to the rather jollier correspondent I sent a copy of the charming poem about St Philip Neri – perhaps the first clerical clown:

> Two books he read with great affection
> The Gospels and a joke collection!
> And sang hosannas set to fiddles
> And fed the sick on soup and riddles.
>
> So when the grave rebuke the merry
> Let them remember Philip Neri
> (1515 to 95)
> Who was the merriest man alive
> Then dying at 80 or a bit,
> Became a saint by holy wit.

The professionally religious have always been a subject for humour. Montalenbert, in *Monks of the*

10

West, quite rightly points out that the Church has always sought certain qualities of its clergy: simplicity, benignity and... HILARITY! The formalized nature of Christian worship has involved man's emotions through drama, solemnity and ritual. The minister to a certain extent has conformed to these requirements and in some cases exaggerated them; in so doing, he has taken the inevitable step from drama to comedy. It is not without significance, I think, that the English theatre was born in the liturgical drama of the thirteenth and fourteenth centuries. In fact, it is curiously satisfying to observe that the first stock comic character in the English theatrical tradition was Mrs Noah, the nagging wife, who was always berating Mr Noah about not looking after the animals properly and inadequately mucking out. Mrs Noah was always played by a monk in drag, and thus the character has remained with us right up until the present day as the pantomime dame.

TRUE HUMILITY
Right Reverend Host. 'I'M AFRAID YOU'VE GOT A BAD EGG, MR. JONES!'
The Curate. 'OH NO, MY LORD, I ASSURE YOU! PARTS OF IT ARE EXCELLENT!'

Within the book you will find an accumulation of stories that I have gathered together as I have made my rounds opening Catholic carnivals, Baptist bazaars, Methodist missions and so on, with of course the occasional bar mitzvah thrown in. Some of the stories you will have heard before – a great many I hope you have not.

The first cartoon which *Punch* has kindly allowed us to reproduce is, for me, particularly important. It is G. du Maurier's celebrated curate's egg drawing. When I was first asked to play the Bishop's Chaplain in *All Gas and Gaiters*, I was a little uncertain how to approach the part. This drawing was then produced for my inspection. The part became clear! His Lordship's guest became the equally humble Mervyn Noote. I hope that you will find that my little collection, unlike Mr Jones's egg, is acceptable all the way through.

FATHER HEAR THY CHILDREN

When it comes to going to church and sorting out where you stand in the sight of your Maker, there must be a lot of grown-ups who find themselves wandering about on pretty stony ground. This probably goes some way towards explaining why they feel almost as uncomfortable faced with their children under these circumstances and why the cosy bedtime chat about God, faith and the great hereafter often comes a close second in the embarrassment stakes to that other subject of eternal questioning, 'Where did I come from?' And here, of course, the biological and the theological are twinned in a frightful compromise of blushing confusion. But I digress.

Many children seem to feel on very easy terms with the Lord and show a touching concern for His well-being, like the little girl who was overheard confiding in her evening prayers, 'Please bless and take care of Mummy and Daddy, and my little brother Alex – and please, God, do take care of yourself. Because if anything happens to you, we're sunk.'

Frankness is the hallmark of the prayers of many children. There was the little boy staying away from home with his parents for the weekend, who found himself all alone in a strange bedroom and offered up this proposal, 'Oh, Lord, don't let anyone hurt me, and I'll go to church on Sunday ... and give you more than two pence.'

Self-preservation lay at the heart of another little penitent's request: 'And, God, please make Bobby stop throwing stones at me. By the way, Lord, I've mentioned this before.'

Children are also free of the nagging scruples about asking for things they want, which afflict so many adults. 'Dear Lord,' prayed one five year old, 'please try and put vitamins and calories in sweets and ice-cream and not just in spinach and cod liver oil.' Another, repeating our Lord's Prayer, insisted on varying the divine text by saying, 'Give us this day our daily oranges.' When gently corrected and told to say 'bread' his answer was, 'No, I've got plenty of bread. What I want is oranges.'

Downright calculating was the little fellow, no doubt heading for a career in politics, who yelled, 'Please, God, bring me a big box of chocolates for my birthday,' to which his mother answered, 'There's no need to shout, dear! God isn't deaf.' 'No, but Grandpa is and he's in the next room,' came the reply. Not that the spiritual and physical appetites need always be at odds in children's prayers, as this nine year old confirmed: 'Please, God, make me like Readybrek - ready to serve.'

It's in trying to instruct children in the fundamentals of the faith that many parents come unstuck. A four year old asked to say his grace before a meal refused to on the grounds that his mother hadn't said hers, to which he added the awful impeachment, 'Mummy never does anything God tells her to.' Then there was the little boy who was asked at Sunday school if he said his prayers at night and who answered, 'No, Mummy does it for me. She says, "Thank God you're in bed at last."' 'Please watch over Daddy,' a little girl, whose father was away, said earnestly, and then added as an afterthought, '...and you'd better keep an eye on Mummy as well.'

Perhaps the best example of this relaxed attitude to the Almighty came from the eight-year-old boy who was asked in a religious education class, 'Why do we say "Amen" at the end of our prayers?' After a moment's reflection he suggested, 'It's a special way of saying "Over and out" to God.'

H.L. Mencken once commented, 'A Sunday school is a prison in which children do penance for the evil conscience of their parents', which might account for some of the unexpected and unorthodox interpretations of the faith that they come out with, from the little boy who was asked, 'Can anyone tell me why you come to Sunday school?' and who answered, 'Because they only have it on Sunday', to the little girl who was visiting London for the first time with her parents and, hearing the Dean's voice coming through a loudspeaker while they were looking round Westminster Abbey during a service, asked excitedly, 'Is that God?'

The arrival of a baby girl, whose mother had described her lovingly as a gift from God, prompted her elder brother to ask, 'Come on, tell me quickly before you forget – what's God like?' Unlike the child busy drawing a picture of God, who answered her mother's comment, 'But no one knows what God looks like, darling,' with, 'No, but they will do when I have finished.'

This matter-of-fact exchange took place between two children comparing their progress in a catechism class. 'I've got to original sin,' bragged one. 'How far have you got to?' 'Me?' said the other. 'I'm way beyond redemption.' Which echoes a similar display of rivalry between two little girls cast in their school's nativity play: 'I'm going to be the virgin,' one of them announced proudly. 'That's nothing,' the other scoffed, 'I'm an angel.' Indignantly, her companion retorted, 'Well, it's much harder to be a virgin' – which raises the matter of the actual interpretation of the Bible and its stories.

Let's start with the Holy Family, the significance of which clearly has still to penetrate some young minds, like that of the prep school boy who asked his drama master eagerly, 'Please, sir, what's this year's Nativity Play about, sir?' Others adopt a more prosaic approach, explaining the circumstances of our Lord's birth in phrases like, 'Well, I blame Joseph, Miss. He should have booked ahead.'

Then there's the fundamentalist line, where concentration on the words rather than the sense of Holy Writ can often be misleading, causing at least one child to assert that Joseph was told to take Mary and the baby and a *flea* to Egypt.

The story of Adam and Eve offers its own pitfalls including the mistaken belief of one child that, 'They were ever so naughty,' adding, when asked what sin they had committed, 'They pinched an apple.' Or the equally original interpretation that the punishment for original sin was to be 'expelled from Eton'.

Innocent confusion reigns about other Old Testament stories. Take for instance one boy's account of the career of the prophet Elijah: 'Elijah was a great prophet. He went for a cruise with a widow.' Or this stimulating discussion that followed a reading of the story of Joseph in a scripture lesson:

> 'What great crime did these sons of Jacob commit?' asked the teacher.
> 'They sold their brother, Joseph,' came the crisp reply.
> 'Quite right. And for how much?'
> 'Twenty pieces of silver,' answered another sharp-witted boy.
> 'And what added to the cruelty and wickedness of these bad brothers?'
> Silence reigned.
> Trying another tack the teacher asked, 'What made their treachery even more detestable and heinous?'
> Another silence followed before a hand shot up and its owner answered breathlessly, 'Please, sir. They sold him too cheap.'

Christ's own work has been the subject of some colourful and intriguing analysis in school classrooms. The parable of the prodigal son was once summed up neatly by a ten year old's account: 'As soon as this shy son was come, he devoured the living calf that killed the fatted harlots.' A girl, asked by her scripture teacher how we know that St Peter repented his denial of

Christ, answered confidently, 'Because he crowed three times.' While a twelve year old took a critical look at our Lord's work and concluded, 'It's just as well Jesus isn't living now. They'd never crucify him. They'd just put him on probation for six months and that would have spoiled all his plans.'

Written examples of this earnest pursuit of fresh insight have a charm of their own. We all have our favourites and here I offer a selection of some that have made me smile over the years:

Noah's wife was called Joan of Ark.

Henry VIII thought so much of Wolsey that he made him a cardigan.

The Fifth Commandment is 'Humour thy father and mother'.

A deacon is a mass of inflammable material.

Lot's wife was a pillar of salt by day ... but a ball of fire by night.

Acrimony (sometimes called 'Holy') is another name for marriage.

Christians can only have one wife. This is called monotony.

A parable is a heavenly story with no earthly meaning.

The Pope lives in a vacuum.

The Pharisees fasted in public, but in private they devoured widows' houses.

Today wild beasts are confined to Theological Gardens.

The patron saint of travellers is St Francis of the sea sick.

A republican is a sinner mentioned in the Bible.

Abraham begat Isaac, and Isaac begat Jacob, and Jacob begat twelve partridges. (A brave and inspired attempt this: see Acts, 7.8)

The natives of Macedonia did not believe, so St Paul got stoned.

The first commandment was when Eve told Adam to eat the apple.

It is sometimes difficult to hear what is being said in church because the agnostics are so terrible.

I also enjoy the story of the little boy whose grandmother gave him a teddy-bear for his birthday and asked him what he intended calling it. He studied the bear gravely before saying, 'I'm going to call it Gladly, Granny, after that bear in the hymn.' 'Which hymn is that?' she asked with some surprise. 'The one that goes "Gladly my cross-eyed bear".'

I myself experienced some confusion as a very small child. Each night before I went to bed I was bidden to kneel down and recite:

Gentle Jesus, meek and mild,
Look upon a little child,
And pity my simplicity
Suffer me to come to Thee

One never questioned this particular entreaty, although I must confess that while I could quite understand the Good Lord being rather enthusiastic regarding 'mice', I never dared to ask what 'plicity' might be.

The lessons of the scriptures themselves can sometimes throw up novel responses. A teacher who asked his class, 'What can we learn from the story of David and Goliath?' was given the reply, 'Please, sir - to duck.'

The nature of Heaven is also open to debate judging from some children's observations. Leaving aside the child who was asked, 'Don't you want to know about Heaven?' and answered, 'No, I want it to be a surprise', consider the case of the little girl who was told that if she was good she would go to Heaven and live with the angels when she died, and showed a refreshingly candid grasp of redemption by asking whether, if she was very good, they would let her have a little devil to play with.

A teacher who had devoted a whole lesson to the subject of repentance ended by summing up her main points and asking her pupils what was the first essential before we could expect forgiveness. 'We must sin, Miss,' was the answer she got. That recalls the answer of a child who was asked if there was any place where God couldn't be found, to which he replied, 'Yes, in the thoughts of the wicked.'

A little boy tucking into a snack before bed was suddenly struck by the thought of the Lord's presence, which prompted the anxious enquiry, 'God can't see me having my supper, can he, Mum?' 'Yes, dear,' she told him, 'God can see everything.' 'But isn't God having his own supper?' 'No, God doesn't need to have any supper, silly.' There was a pause that ended with the cheerful realization, 'No, I suppose he has an egg with his tea.'

Move the action on a couple of scenes and we come to bedtime, prayers and fond goodnight wishes. 'Cover yourself up, darling,' said a doting mother on a chilly night, 'the angels will keep you warm.' Unconvinced, her young son asked, 'I don't suppose I could change my angel for a hot-water bottle?'

There is a refreshing naturalness about the reply given by the little girl who was asked by a visiting preacher who had made her. 'God made me so long,' she answered, holding up her hands to indicate her length at birth, 'but the rest I grew myself.'

Like parents, the clergy can often find the candour of youthful faith unsettling at times. One vicar who was rash enough to ask one of his Sunday school pupils if there was anything he would like to have explained was asked, 'What is a miracle?' Trying to give a straightforward answer, the vicar explained miracles in a few short sentences and felt well pleased with his

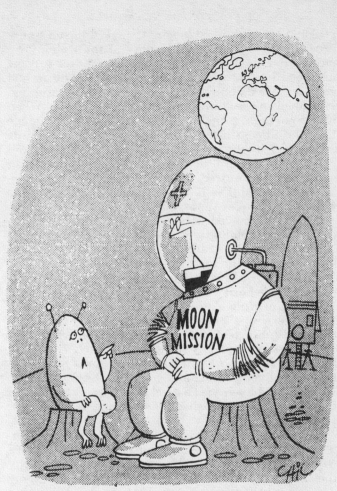

'...and all this time we thought God lived up there!'

account. 'Now do you understand what a miracle is?' he concluded. 'Yes, but it's not my mum's idea of a miracle. Whenever she knows you're calling at our house she says it will be a miracle if you don't stay for tea.'

Bishop King of Lincoln found himself once experiencing the practical reality of the well-known phrase from the Bible, 'Suffer the little children to come unto me.' Staying with friends near Folkestone, he had gone for a walk one warm summer morning and had lain down on the shingly beach to enjoy the sun. When it came to getting up, however, his rheumatism made the effort impossible and he was obliged to call a little girl playing by the water to help him. 'This is very kind of you, my dear. But do you really think you're strong enough?' he enquired. 'Oh yes,' answered the child, taking his arm, 'I've often helped my daddy when he was much drunker than you.'

Equally open-eyed was the answer of another little girl to another bishop who asked her what was the best preparation for 'the sacrament of holy matrimony'. 'A little courting,' she answered brightly.

'Suffering' little children can tax the most accomplished of the Lord's anointed at times. During his term as Bishop of Winchester, Samuel Wilberforce (of whom more later), was once walking down Windsor High Street with his host, the Dean of Windsor, when they came across a small boy struggling to reach a doorbell. Seeing that help was needed, Wilberforce offered to ring the bell for him. 'Thank you,' said the boy politely. Wilberforce duly gave it a good pull. The boy beamed in approval and then dashed off shouting, 'Now, mister, run like hell!'

It was the little daughter of the Dean of Peterborough, Dr Saunders, who once asked Wilberforce with childish simplicity, 'Will you tell me, Bishop, why they call you "Soapy Sam"?' 'I am afraid I can't, my dear,' he said benignly, 'unless it's because I am always in hot water, but come up with clean hands.'

Bishop Harvey Goodwin of Carlisle offered an explanation every bit as appealing to a little girl who showed intense interest in his pastoral staff. He'd been staying with one of his rectors, and leaving the house with his luggage, he spotted the child staring fixedly at the case in which the staff was packed. With time to spare before catching his train, he unpacked the staff, put it together and showed it to her, saying, 'You see, the point is to push on those of the clergymen in my diocese who don't go fast enough, and the crook is to keep back those who go too fast.'

No such explanation was required by the boy at prep school who wrote to his parents:

> Dear Mum and Dad,
> Last week the bishop came for confirmation. I had a good view of him from where I sat in the chapel and now I know what a crook really looks like.

Church ceremonials hold other mysteries as shown by the child who attended his first service and, after watching the surpliced procession of the vicar and choir during the first hymn, asked in a penetrating voice, 'Daddy, are they all going to have their hair cut?'

Similar confusion reigned in the mind of the little girl who was acting as a bridesmaid for the first time and asked the bride anxiously about the vicar, 'He isn't going to give me an injection is he?'

The nature of different ceremonies can cause bewilderment too. A child who attended a christening one Sunday, went to a wedding the following week and asked her mother during one of the periods of private prayer, 'Mummy - where's the baby?' Which is matched only by the four year old who was so excited by the news that his Mummy had been given a baby by God and was keeping it under her heart until it was big enough to be born, that he proclaimed his thanks loudly during the hush of silent prayer the following Sunday, saying, 'Thank you, God, for giving my Mummy a baby, but she's keeping it under her *hat* until it's bigger.'

Not long after a birth in another family the parish priest called at the house and said to the eldest daughter, 'I hear God has brought you two lovely twin brothers.' 'Yes,' she said proudly, 'and what's more He knows where their school fees will be coming from – I heard Daddy saying so.'

In circumstances like these it can be helpful to remember the interdiction from the Ten Commandments when the Good Lord warns about 'visiting the iniquity of the fathers upon the children'.

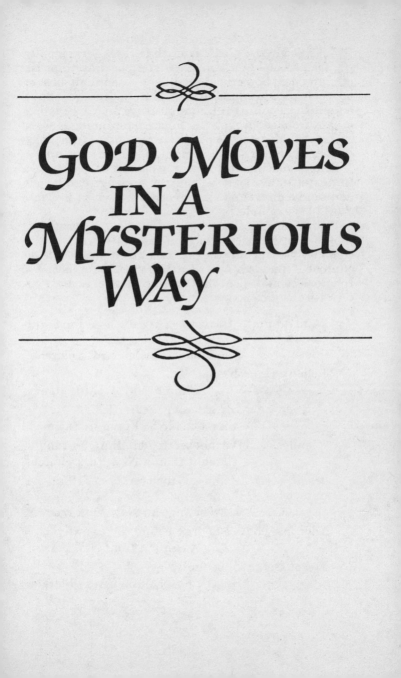

GOD MOVES IN A MYSTERIOUS WAY

It isn't always God's fault that He is occasionally seen to move in a more mysterious way than He intended. Sometimes (and more often than most of us would care to admit), it's we, His children, who have a hand in clouding the Divine message or in distracting others from it through the misunderstandings, slips, errors and bloomers to which we are prone. To err may be human, but it's also humorous in many instances.

Before focusing on how wrong church people can get things at times, let's see how the message can be put across in a direct and unequivocal way – as in the New World for example.

There's a refreshing openness about attitudes to religion in America which is most apparent to the casual observer in the signs and notices outside churches. Here is a selection that gives a flavour of a religious commitment that rolls up its sleeves and gets on with the job:

Want to go to Heaven?... Apply here for flight training.

Church noticeboard, Colorado.

Bellev_e Church needs 'U'.

Church noticeboard, Maine.

Come in now and get your faith lifted.

Sign outside a church in St Louis.

A smile is a curve that sets a lot of things straight.

Thought from a New York church.

Jesus saves... and at today's prices that's a miracle!

From another New York church.

Your last chance to pray before the freeway.

A caution from New Jersey.

Trespassers will be forgiven.

Absolution from Florida.

Church parking only. Offenders will be baptized.

Notice outside a New England church.

Prayers have to be notified on the correct form or they will not be processed.

Notice in a Kansas church.

The art of the parable still has its place in American worship none the less. A New York Methodist minister once felt compelled to place this advertisement in one of the city's newspapers:

Lost, Stolen or Strayed. A large flock of Methodist sheep. They have been gone for some time. When last seen they were browsing along the road of indifference. Anyone finding these sheep please bring them home, if possible, and you will receive ample reward. If they refuse to come home drive them to the nearest fold, lock the door, and report to the undersigned. Plenty of fodder will be provided on Sunday.

So much for the message that comes across loud and clear. See the difference that a little interference can make – again starting with an example from the States, taken from a notice given out by an Episcopalian church in Maryland, 'Thursday at 3.30 p.m. there will be an Ice Cream Social. All ladies giving milk please come early.'

Graffiti artists are no respecters of sanctity and church notices frequently lend themselves to their imagination and embellishment, as these examples show:

Jesus Saves! – With the Woolwich.

Jesus Saves! – But Moses headed it in off the post.

Jesus Saves! – Save yourself. Jesus is tired.

Love Your Enemies – And they'll wonder what kind of deal you're trying to pull.

Work for God – The fringe benefits are out of this world.

27

Where will you be on the day of judgement? – Still waiting for the number 83 bus.

Tired of Sin? – If not ring...

In six days the Lord made heaven and earth, the sea and all that is in them – He was self-employed.

Other elements of religious life also inspire their work. A newspaper poster outside a newsagent's in Coventry carried the caption ͵'Choirboy caught betting', beneath which had been scrawled, 'Ah – those sweet childish trebles.'

'Thank God for atheism,' proclaimed an evangelist's message in metallic blue spray-paint. 'Get the Abbey Habit,' read one of that building society's posters, to which someone had added, 'Sleep with a monk.' Another, carefully recorded on the wall of a university library lavatory read:

Jesus said to them, 'Who do you say that I am?' They replied, 'You are the eschatological manifestation of the ground of our being, the kerygma of which we find the ultimate meaning in our inter-personal relationships.' And Jesus said, 'What?'

Frequently much innocent humour comes from the charmingly ambiguous signs and notices that appear in parish magazines and pinned to noticeboards all over the country.

Let's take the notices first. Here's a vicar from Surrey writing in his parish magazine: 'The bishop will preach here next Sunday and his wife will open our annual garden fête on the following Saturday. On both occasions I hope to be away on holiday.'

Another, commenting in his monthly letter to his parishioners on a recent debate by the Church of England's governing body, wrote, 'It appears the General Synod found the debate on "Sex" rather an embarrassing subject, which just goes to show how our

'He can't be getting at us. He hardly knows us.'

elected members can so easily miss a chance to make the best of an opportunity.'

'We are thinking of forming a branch of the Mother's Union in the parish,' wrote an elderly rector to his congregation, 'so any ladies wishing to become mothers should meet me in the vestry after the service.'

A recently arrived incumbent informed his flock in his first piece in the parish newsletter, 'The vicar wishes it to be known that as the parish is very scattered it will be some time before he is able to visit all his new parishioners, and this no doubt will be appreciated by them.'

It was a literal interpretation of the word 'flock' that must have caused a few double-takes at a notice from Hampshire that informed readers, 'In an effort to enlist volunteers to help with maintaining the churchyard it has been divided into five areas. One will be grazed by the vicar's sheep and it is hoped that at least three or four human volunteers will be found to take care of the others.'

Confusion may have reigned over another churchyard following this announcement: 'On the dedication Sunday the procession to the churchyard will take place in the afternoon. If it rains in the afternoon, the procession will be held in the morning.'

Announcements about services don't always mean what they say either. Shortly after a PCC decided to drop evensong the vicar wrote enthusiastically, 'More people are now attending the 11.30 service than used to attend the two services when there was one.'

Whereas the statement written elsewhere, 'The revised service will begin at 10.30 and will continue until further notice', was guaranteed to frighten off all but the most stalwart parishioners. As was the Holy Week notice, 'Evensong will be said at 8.00 p.m., and a sermon preached from Monday till Friday inclusive.' Unlike the notice that appeared outside a Baptist church, 'Instead of the usual service, there will be a Pleasant Hour at 7.00 p.m.'

Special events in the life of the Church invite their own misunderstandings. A weekend conference held to discuss the Church's response to famine contained this intriguing programme:

30

3.00	Hymns of praise
	Films
3.45	'Hungry Men'
4.15	Question Time
4.30	Tea and Buns (50p per person)
5.00	'I was hungry – sick'
5.45	'What do we do?'
	Open forum
6.45	Prayers

So do special appeals, like this one: 'The Minister is going on holiday at the end of next week. Could all Missionary Boxes be handed into the Manse by Friday evening at the latest.' And this, 'We regret to announce that the "Ladies Happy Hour" is now heavily in debt following the recent Sponsored Silence.'

More cheerful news was brought to one parish by its sacristan who chose to inform his fellow-parishioners that their much loved, but equally elderly, rector had recovered from an illness, by displaying the notice outside their church, 'God is good. The rector is better.'

Unfortunately, the same happy tidings could not be spread to members of a church in Sheffield, to whom their vicar had to write, 'The healing service to be held next Sunday will be taken by myself. The healer, who was to have come, has gone into hospital for an operation.'

A visitor to a parish in Essex was promised a rather different form of reception by the notice that heralded his arrival: 'The Rev Andrew Adano, a nomad priest from North Kenya, will be coming to Danbury next Sunday for a week's stay at the Rectory. Anyone wishing to have him for a meal during his stay should ask the Rector, please.'

Equally dismissive was the notice that read, 'Jumble Sale next Saturday morning. (This is a good chance to get rid of anything that is not worth keeping.) Don't forget to bring your husbands along.'

It isn't only the clergy or those who write in parish magazines who create these engaging *faux pas*. The press belong to the same worthy tradition. From East Anglia comes this account of one ecclesiastical gathering: 'The sudden gust of wind took all who were at the ceremony by surprise. Hats were blown off and copies of the vicar's speech and other rubbish were scattered over the site.' In another part of the country an estate agent offered, 'Chapel, suitable for conversion. All main services.' While a perfectly innocent, but no less appealing, entry in the *Wiltshire Gazette* read: 'The donkey failed to arrive for the Palm Sunday procession at St Peter's Church Chippenham. The procession was led by the Vicar, the Revd Jeremy Bray.'

More permanent than any of these are the signs that decorate churches, bearing words of wisdom intended to endure beyond the immediate matters in hand. You can often find these in churchyards, where signs such as 'Persons are prohibited from picking flowers from any but their own graves' and 'Anyone having relatives buried in this churchyard is asked to be so good as to keep them in order' go a long way in emphasizing the proximity of our earthly existence the other only just around the corner.

'Don't let worry kill you off – Let the Church help' read another comforting message that stood outside a North London church, and for any who might have felt moved to follow its advice the sign on a church door elsewhere in the great metropolis might have raised doubts: 'This is the Gate of Heaven, enter ye all by this door', it beckoned, below which was a note reading, 'This door is kept locked because of the draught.'

Generally speaking, church signs rely on an eye-catching, thought-provoking message to draw worshippers inside. There is the matter-of-fact approach of the one that read:

When you were born, your mother brought you
here,
When you were married, your partner brought you
here,
When you die your friends will bring you here,
Why not try coming on your own sometimes?

Or the suggestion outside a church in Newcastle:
'Pray now and avoid the Christmas rush.'

An enterprising vicar in a country parish much
favoured by ramblers, cyclists and canoeists distributed
details of his services to youth hostels, pubs and cafés
in the area which ended with the invitation: 'We will be
glad to see you at any of our services – Clothes don't
matter.'

Invitations with a touch of menace can be striking
too. 'What is hell like?' asked one large sign outside a
church in Liverpool, under which was another reading,
'Come and hear our choir.' In Southampton the
missionary zeal of one of the city's churches led to the
erection of a sign with far-reaching implications:
'Wanted – Workers for God – Plenty of overtime.'

In the face of inner-city decay and depression there
are many churches that take a defiantly optimistic line
in calling inside God's errant sheep. Appealing to
man's mercenary instincts one read: 'Prayer, the only
commodity not going up.'

A strong evangelical sense must have inspired the
creators of the one that advised, 'The only useful thing
to do with good advice is to pass it on. It is never any use
to oneself.'

Lastly there are those matter-of-fact signs, similar to
dozens of others seen in public places asking us either
to do or not to do certain things, but which phrased in
the primarily religious context with which we're
concerned here have a reverence and dignity that
elevates them above the humdrum. Take the simple
matter of where you leave your car. What could be more

fitting than the request outside a church in East Anglia: 'Pray, do not park here'? And how about the mystical excitement engendered by the straightforward request to ring a doorbell, which appeared outside the home of a spiritualist: 'Please ring the bell. Knocking only confuses things.' Or the ominous forebodings raised by, 'No healing during August.'

Unfortunately, it's this same reverence and dignity that makes the Church so vulnerable to the innocent slips that occasionally occur in transferring ideas to print – slips that in other areas of life might pass almost unnoticed.

The typist responsible for preparing notices and hymn sheets in one church hit the wrong key while typing the words of a hymn with the result that instead of reading, '... be sure, he bids you', it was presented to the congregation as 'be sure he beds you'. On a similar theme was the announcement in a parish magazine that accidentally appeared as, 'A special service of thanksgiving for the success of the recent campaign in aid of distressed daughters of the Clergy will be held on Thursday evening at 7.00 p.m. and will be followed by mating in the Church Hall.'

The graffiti on a church notice that read, 'No connection with the Post Office. Two collections every Sunday', reminds us that that hallowed body is not without its hiccups. Twenty years ago, when Dr Coggan was Archbishop of York, he ran a campaign that encouraged church workers to go out and meet people in every walk of life. The caption for this scheme was 'Opportunity Unlimited', and stickers carrying this message went out on all church correspondence. At the same time other tidings were being spread far and wide from York – the dates of the May race meeting, which the York race committee had paid the Post Office to stamp on all the letters leaving the city. The upshot was that all over the diocese church workers received mail in envelopes that bore the message, 'Opportunity

Unlimited... York Races May 18, 19 and 20.' Any
doubts that might have been raised by this were
dispelled as soon as the mistake was spotted and Dr
Coggan had issued a statement that neatly distinguished between the spiritual and the temporal.
'There is opportunity unlimited to lose money at York
Races,' he wrote. 'There is opportunity unlimited to win
life in this diocesan movement. As Dick Turpin often
said on his way to York, it is a case of your money or
your life.'

It can happen that the message from the past isn't
always carried into the present with as clear a meaning
as this, as one of Dr Coggan's fellow bishops discovered
in a tea-shop where, dressed in gaiters and apron, he
had enjoyed a very good tea. When the waitress
presented him with the bill and collected his payment,
she asked him to sign it, so that she could keep it as a
souvenir. This he willingly did adding a cross in
episcopal style as he habitually did. 'Oh, how sweet of
you,' said the girl. 'And with a kiss as well!'

Even the printed message in the Bible hasn't always
been spared human error in its preparation, let alone
interpretation. In 1631 Robert Barker and Martin
Lucas, printers in London to King Charles I, printed a
thousand copies of an edition of the Bible that
contained one notable error – somehow the word 'not'
had been left out of the seventh commandment with the
result that countless readers would have found
apparent support for their fun and games outside (and
occasionally inside) the nuptial bed, had not the entire
print run been withdrawn from the market. And the
wording? 'Thou shalt commit adultery', which has led
it to be called The Wicked Bible ever since!

Even correctly printed, Holy Writ can present
unexpected challenges to those who take it into foreign
lands. A missionary working in Accra experienced
some difficulty in translating the key phrase, 'I am the
good shepherd,' since there were no sheep to be seen

anywhere in the country. His interpreter was also at a loss and finally settled on the rather more prosaic rendering, 'The minister says he is a good man who has some goats.'

Though that does at least give some indication to the listeners of what was meant, unlike much of the florid language that has sometimes decorated ecclesiastical speech. One rector urged his flock to 'tread the straight and narrow path where only one can walk abreast'. Another offering advice to a young man about to make his way in the world cautioned, 'You will often come face to face with people who have lost their heads.'

There was a preacher who denounced the husband who spent all his evenings drinking in the pub, 'while his poor wife rocks the cradle with one foot and wipes her eyes with the other.'

A curate in Scotland reassured his congregation, 'The ship of the Church can never be wrecked, for it is founded on a rock.' And a speaker addressing a church meeting on behalf of a new missionary society told his listeners, 'I must confess, brethren, that our work is in an early stage; but I do claim that we have driven in the thin end of the wedge, and devoutly hope that ere long we may leaven the whole lump.' Make of those what you will.

There's little wonder that some of God's anointed have difficulty in winning over a congregation or a parish when you consider what they occasionally allow themselves to write and say. A clergyman who had worked for many years in a parish in the Isle of Wight eventually left for a distant benefice in the North. He still kept in touch with his former congregation, however, and on his first return assured them of his pleasure in seeing 'so many old Cowes' faces' looking up at him.

Writing in his parish magazine, one vicar observed, 'We have been most fortunate this year with our choirmaster and organist. Both have been given

36

appointments that will take them from us.'

A potential increase in church membership might have been nipped in the bud by a decision of the incumbent of an inner-city parish, who announced that 'an additional font will be placed in the church, so that babies can be baptized at both ends'.

And the Reverend A. Saint wrote to *The Times* once to tell of the time when he was introduced to the people of a new parish as 'our new vicar, Mr Satan'. Though even this pales into insignificance when we consider the delightful ambiguity aroused by the name of the Archbishop of Manila, Cardinal Sin.

Just occasionally little slips of the devout can be extraordinarily perceptive or apposite. The elderly rector of a country parish in the West Country, praying shortly after the Armistice in 1918, asked his Maker for 'that world which the peace cannot give'.

Twenty years later, when broadcasting was starting to make a real impression on the world, the minister leading a church service that was being transmitted down the airwaves, prayed, 'Lord, there are those afflicted by the radio today; comfort them, we ask Thee.'

An admiral arriving late in the Mess for dinner, looked round the table, took in those present and then delivered the customarily brief naval grace with the words, 'No chaplain? Thank God.' While a junior officer in command of a destroyer that was returning to port after taking part in anti-submarine exercises, sent a signal to his fellow-commander on board the sub asking if he was getting bored with always being the target. Taking the opportunity to express his true feelings without voicing them to the fleet at large, he radioed back, 'Hebrews, 13.8' ('Jesus Christ, the same yesterday, and today and for ever').

Diplomats, of course, are trained in the art of saying one thing and meaning another; a pleasing example of this is told of the days when Lord Curzon ruled the

Foreign Office. At that time it would appear that the FO exercised some control over the monks on Mt Athos in northern Greece. Be that as it may, one day a telegram arrived announcing, 'The monks of Mt Athos have violated their vows.' Curzon, however, misread this, transposed a 'c' for a 'v' and took it to mean, 'The monks of Mt Athos have violated their cows.' Someone had written across it, 'No doubt caused by a Papal Bull', to which Curzon added, 'A mere clerical error.'

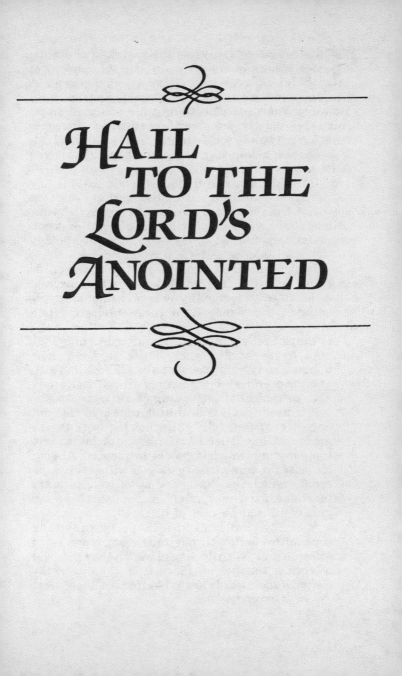

HAIL TO THE LORD'S ANOINTED

The way the clergy see their work in the wider world doesn't always tie in with the opinions of the laity. To Ambrose Bierce a clergyman was 'A man who undertakes the management of our spiritual affairs as a method of bettering his temporal ones.' Unlike the elderly priest who eventually agreed to retire, but not before suggesting to God, 'O Lord, if I can no longer be a labourer in your vineyard, will you please use me in an advisory capacity.'

Anglican clergy are frequently mocked for the metaphors and allusions with the spiritual life that they draw from the most prosaic of everyday objects, but one of the neatest illustrations of what makes a successful parson must surely come from the analogy with a teapot that dates from the last century.

The teapot was presented by a bishop to one of his clergy on behalf of the parishioners whom he had served devotedly for many years. In making his presentation the bishop drew these interesting parallels:

> Perhaps I may point out to you some details that may have escaped your notice to show how appropriately your friends have selected this gift, and the useful lessons you may draw from a study of it; as typical of the calling of a clergyman.
>
> It is useful as it is beautiful, that is to say, not only does it faithfully carry out the work it was made for, but it lends charm and a joy to any company into which it may be introduced. Among its most prominent features you will observe the spout, which discharges one of the primary functions, for what flows from it should cheer and gratify all that partake of it.
>
> Again, you will remember that before anything is permitted to flow through the spout, a process of infusion must silently take place. The same should be true of that which flows from the lips of the clergy; if their words are to be effective, there must

be a short period of thoughtful preparation.

The lid is another prominent feature, illustrating the importance of being able to 'shut up' at the right time.

You should also appreciate that what flows from the teapot does not originate there; it is only the instrument, the means, the channel. The water must be drawn from the eternal source and it must be pure. Sometimes, too, the plain truth will not be accepted by everyone who partakes of it until it has been sweetened or mixed with the milk of human kindness.

You may also notice something that is not ostentatiously paraded, though it will always be found by those looking carefully for it, and that is the stamp of its Maker. A clergyman declares himself to be an ambassador of Christ, and in the true ambassador the credentials are always to be discerned.

Finally, in some mysterious way, age confers a higher beauty and value, and, although perhaps infirm in places, there is a sanctity and reverence that Time alone can confer on vessels decrepit with service.

Perhaps that's why the vicar of so many jokes is always being offered 'more tea'.

Bishop Blomfield once chose to render a charge to his clergy in verse and each received the instructions:

Hunt not, fish not, shoot not,
Dance not, fiddle not, flute not,
Be sure you have nothing to do with the Whigs,
But stay at home, and feed your pigs;
And above all, I make it my particular desire,
That at least once a week you dine with the Squire.

He showed interest too in the charges delivered by others, enquiring on one occasion what had been the subject of his two archdeacons' charges. One said that it had been the art of making sermons, the other of churchyards. 'I see,' said Blomfield, 'composition and decomposition.'

Qualifications sought from prospective clergymen have varied through the centuries. In the first half of the eighteenth century one newspaper advertisement appeared stating:

> A curate wanted, who will have easy duty and a stipend of £50 per annum, besides valuable perquisites. He must be zealously affected to the present Government, and never forsake his principles, regular in his morals, sober and abstemious, grave in his dress and deportment, choice in his company, and exemplary in his conversation. He must be of superior abilities, studious and careful in his employment of time, a lover of fiddling, but no dancer.

What's interesting is that no mention is made of his calling or how he might be expected to answer it, and as to the direction of his political affinities, there must be many in Whitehall today who would wish for a similar state of affairs.

At the turn of this century the criteria for selecting a vicar for a rural parish had shifted somewhat, but the bedrock of Anglicanism could still be seen below the surface, when the patron of a country benefice advertised for a parson, specifying that he should be a graduate (having if possible passed through the same school as the patron himself), that he should be good with men (whatever that was meant to mean), that he should be musical, tactful and (almost as an after-thought, though it did at least merit a mention) a good preacher. As a coda he added, 'Income, unfortunately not large, but there is a magnificent rectory.' Many replies were received, among them one asked, 'Does it matter if he is not a left-handed bowler?'

Moving nearer our own time, a vicar in need of help

with running his parish adopted a novel way of weeding out candidates right from the advertisement and wrote: 'Assistant Priest wanted. Travelling expenses paid to Caleb the son of Jephunneh.' Those familiar with the Book of Numbers would have remembered that Caleb was one of those who went to view the Promised Land.

In the north of Scotland a candidate for the pulpit of a country church spent a week with the retiring minister, at the end of which he was due. to preach to the congregation at their regular Sunday service. He was anxious to secure the appointment and asked his host what was likely to be the best way of winning the parish's approval. 'Show them as much critical knowledge as you can,' he was told. 'And the more languages you can quote the better they'll like you.' Speaking nothing but English and Welsh, this last point presented the candidate with a problem, but with little option but to do his best he appeared in the pulpit the following Sunday and announced his text at the start of the sermon. Having repeated it, he indicated that the English translation was at fault, adding, 'In the original Hebrew the sentence runs as follows,' and then quoted the line in Welsh. Several grave heads in front of him nodded in approval.

A little later he stopped at another divergence in translation which allowed him to observe, 'To understand this verse we should carefully study the original Aramaic,' before quoting the lines, again in Welsh.

Coming to another passage, in the New Testament, he said, 'The innate loveliness and true sublimity of this beautiful sentence can only be truly appreciated in the Greek,' which he then rendered into Welsh.

So far all had gone to plan. Those who counted themselves scholars looked at each other with smiles of recognition and those who didn't tried to look more earnest as the sermon progressed.

It was only when quoting in Welsh a famous 'Latin' passage that the would-be minister realized that his number was up. Right at the back of the church sat a large, jolly man, who was bursting his sides with laughter. So, changing quickly from the translation of the text in front of him, he said loudly in Welsh, 'My friend, for Heaven's sake! Please don't let anyone know about this until I've had a word with you.' The Welshman nodded in agreement, along with the rest, who were unanimous in electing a man who had a fluent knowledge of the scriptures in five languages.

Not all who receive preferment are held in such respect, of course. Senior clergy in particular seem to have a universally derogatory attitude towards curates. One incumbent summed them up as being, 'Those who have done what they ought not to have done; those who left undone what they ought to have done; and those who have no health in them.'

Then there was the curate who, still a deacon, drew his bishop's attention to the reference in the Benedicite to 'Oh ye priests of the Lord' and expressed his regret that no mention was made of deacons. 'You have overlooked the reference, young man,' replied the bishop, 'the one that reads, "O all ye green things upon the earth."'

The elderly members of the cloth can come in for the same treatment. A bishop attending his enthronement ceremony was standing at the door of his new cathedral and, as is the custom, knocked three times with his staff to be admitted. A long pause followed the knocking and he was about to try again when the huge door swung slowly open and the stately procession of dean, sub-dean and canons, all well advanced in years, made its arthritic way towards him. While they were still out of earshot, the bishop whispered to his chaplain, 'The See gives up its dead.'

Changing jobs can have unexpected coincidences for clergy of all ranks, as Archbishop Alexander found when he was transferred from the See of Derry. The consecration of his successor was fixed for the Feast of St Matthias, which wasn't entirely to the departing Archbishop's liking, since, as he mildly pointed out, the collect for the day was a little unkind to him, reading as it does, 'Who, into the place of the traitor Judas didst set Thy faithful servant Matthias.'

To a non-conformist, however, the calling of an Anglican clergyman to a higher benefice had a perfectly simple explanation: 'While he is praying below for guidance, his wife is upstairs busily packing.'

At the bottom of the ecclesiastical ladder come those who have just been ordained, a process that gives them their first taste of church life from the inside – like how to deal with bishops. Shortly before their actual ordination the ordinands go into retreat to make their final preparations. A former bishop of Lincoln held one once and set aside one afternoon for contemplation and prayer, to which he left the young men in his charge. So it came as a surprise an hour or so later to meet one of his charges walking down the street, to whom he said, 'I was under the impression that I had left you to seek guidance from the Holy Spirit this afternoon.' 'Yes, you did, Your Grace, and the Holy Spirit gave me strict instructions to do my shopping this afternoon and I didn't think I could very well go against that.' 'Well, one of you must be wrong,' said the bishop, 'because it's early closing day.'

Another ordinand being interviewed by another bishop was asked whether he read his Bible every day. 'Certainly I do, Your Grace, every day,' he assured. 'Do you have any plan to your reading?' the bishop asked. 'Yes, I do, Your Grace.' 'Do you follow the Church's calendar and the lessons provided for each day?' 'Not so rigidly, Your Grace.' 'Do you have a scheme of your own, then?' 'Yes, I do, Your Grace.' 'And what is that scheme?' 'It's just a plan of my own. I always read what I think is likely to have some bearing on what's going to happen that day.' 'I see. Well, tell me, what did you read today, for instance?' 'Oh, Your Grace, knowing I was going to see your lordship today, I just read the "Comfortable Words".'

Pragmatism guided the answer of a class of students in a theological college whose tutor asked them whether, given the choice, they would prefer to be with the ten wise virgins in the light or the ten unwise virgins in the dark. Their unanimous answer must have set him wondering whether they were following the right calling, though the comment in a student essay, 'Faith is the faculty by which we are called to believe that which is not true', did at least show a willingness to grapple with the problems facing the Church in the modern world.

During an oral examination Bishop Whatley asked the candidate in front of him what the difference was between a form and a ceremony. There was a pause while the man cudgelled his brains for an answer, but before he could reply Whatley came to his rescue. 'You are right, the meanings to me seem nearly the same, though you must admit there is a very fine distinction all the same; you sit on a form, but you stand on a ceremony.'

Ordination candidates studying under the guidance of a former Bishop of Peterborough were each told to make a very careful study of Bishop Butler's *Analogy of Religion Natural and Revealed*, and each made an earnest note to this effect. Saying goodbye to one of his students, the bishop once remarked, 'Goodbye, my dear young friend,' and then added gravely, 'Whatever you do, don't forget the Butler.' 'Your Grace, I assure you I haven't,' replied the student, 'I have only this minute given him half a crown.'

Junior members of the clergy employ a variety of means in trying to impress their seniors. One curate asked by his bishop what he thought was the greatest challenge facing the modern Church, opted for morality and expressed his disgust at the lack of it. 'Young people today, Your Grace, think nothing of sex before marriage. I never slept with my wife before we were married. Did you, Your Grace?' 'I don't know,' replied the bishop, 'What was her maiden name?'

A clergy wife seldom plays an unsung role in her husband's work. A colonial bishop, corresponding with a colleague in England, made this apparent when he wrote: 'I should like to commend to you the Reverend Robinson who returns to your shores after thirty years devoted service in these colonies. He has been my chaplain since my arrival and I shall feel quite lost without him. I have found him a good visitor, an acceptable preacher, and a devout priest. All I have said about the Reverend Robinson is equally applicable to Mrs Robinson.'

It wouldn't be true to imply that the relationship between bishops and their clergy is always as harmonious as this. One old bishop left a message in verse to his clergy, to be conveyed to them from his Will after his death:

> Tell my priests when I am gone,
> O'er me to shed no tears,
> For I shall be no deader then
> Than they have been for years.

Some young clergy can be too sharp for their own good, of course. One student in a theological college reported to the Principal that he had seen one of the tutors who gave classes in Hebrew working secretly from a translation. 'Is that so?' replied the Principal, 'So the Ass knoweth its master's crib.'

Bishops also have to take an admonitory line with those clergy who allow themselves to be deflected from the path of their true calling by some of their paraphernalia. Bishop Creighton once had to ask one of his London vicars to stop using incense in his services. The vicar replied that it was of vital

importance to his work, emphasizing, 'Your Grace, I am charged with the curing of 10,000 souls.' 'Quite so,' answered the bishop, 'but you don't want to be charged with curing them like so many kippers.'

I've acquired over the years a considerable collection of cartoons of the clergy, mainly by Ape and Spy, and there's one in particular that I always especially enjoy, which is of an Anglican vicar, who, as a ritualist, would only clean the handrail of his church with a consecrated duster.

Other young priests find their enthusiasm blunted by having to work with doddery old colleagues. One elderly rector, devout, but frequently miles away during services, was taking evensong on a lovely summer evening. After leading the Nunc Dimittis he paused before the Creed ... and paused ... and paused. Feet started to shuffle in the congregation and his young curate crossed from his stall to touch his arm and whisper, 'I believe in God, sir.' 'So do I ... so do I,' answered the rector with a happy smile.

If the clergy can have their differences with their colleagues, these are small beer compared with the issues that often divide them from clerics of other denominations. During an ecumenical conference two minor clergy – one Roman Catholic, the other Anglican – got into a heated argument that ranged over four centuries of Church history without reaching any conclusion. Eventually the Roman Catholic priest brought it to an end by saying: 'We really shouldn't quarrel like this. We are both doing God's work after all – you in your way and I in His.'

John Wilkes, the eighteenth-century wit and politician, won a point for the other side in an argument with a Roman Catholic who asked him hotly, 'Where was your religion before the Reformation?' 'Did you wash your face this morning?' asked Wilkes. 'I did, sir.' 'Well then, where was your face before it was washed?' Which is a riposte every bit as appealing as that he gave to a heckler at the hustings who yelled, 'I would rather vote for the devil than for John Wilkes.' 'And if your friend is not standing...?' was Wilkes's calm reply.

Centuries of religious conflict can result in an underlying tension between those of different persuasions. This was the case during a church conference held in Wales, when a group of the delegates took themselves off for a walk to explore the countryside. At one point they reached a stream spanned by a flimsy bridge that carried a notice warning walkers not to use it. They decided to chance their luck all the same, and were inching gingerly across when they heard shouting from across a field and saw a stout man running towards them. 'It's all right,' one of them reassured him as he panted up, not appreciating his concern. 'We are Anglicans from the conference.' 'That's your concern,' said the man, 'but if you don't get off that bridge sharpish you'll all be Baptists.'

One of the commonest arguments against religious belief is that it frequently runs contrary to the rational, analytical basis on which so much contemporary knowledge and thought is based. A philosopher and theologian were locked in just such a confrontation, in which the theologian stated the traditional argument that the philosopher was like a blind man in a darkened room, looking for a black cat that wasn't there. 'That's all very well,' countered the philosopher, 'but a theologian would have found it.'

This exchange was echoed by one between a clergyman and a doctor, who in practising deism acknowledged the existence of God, but rejected the revelation and supernatural doctrines of Christianity. The doctor kicked off by asking if the parson had taken to his work to save souls. The parson replied that he had. Had he ever seen a soul? No. Had he ever heard a soul? No. Had he ever smelt a soul? No. Had he ever tasted a soul? No. Then, had he ever felt a soul? 'Yes,' answered the clergyman, with relief. 'All right,' said the doctor, 'but four of the five senses suggest that there isn't a soul.'

Now it was the clergyman's turn and he asked the doctor if he considered himself a doctor of medicine. Of course he did, he answered. 'In that case,' asked the clergyman, 'have you ever heard a pain?' The doctor hadn't. Had he ever smelt a pain? No. Had he ever tasted a pain? No. Had he ever seen a pain? The doctor had to admit that he hadn't. Had he ever felt a pain? That he certainly had, he retorted. 'All right,' said the clergyman, 'but that still leaves four of the five senses confirming that there is no such thing as a pain; and yet, you know that there is a pain, and I know that there is a soul.'

A preacher at a large open-air service scored an outright winner by employing similar tactics against a man who persisted in mocking his address on religious faith on the ground that no one who regarded himself as an intellectual could believe in anything he couldn't see. In the end the clergyman tackled him directly and asked whether he had any brains. 'I most certainly have,' retorted the heckler, 'and it's because of them that I stand by what I say.' 'Have you ever seen your brains?' asked the clergyman next. After that his sermon was allowed to continue without interruption.

Faced with a constant barrage of intellectual challenges to their faith, it isn't surprising that some clergy occasionally lapse into depression. One preacher who was prone to this used to revive his spirits by the memory of the evangelist, Billy Sunday, who, told that the effect of his revivalist services didn't last, replied cheerfully, 'Neither does a bath, but it does you good to take one.'

Differences in custom can cause as great a difficulty between different denominations, as an English vicar travelling in a very devout part of Scotland found in the last century. Having been told that there wouldn't be any hot water for him to shave with on a Sunday morning, he got round the problem by ordering some hot grog and giving the whisky to the man who brought it.

Ecclesiastical clothes bring about misunderstandings too. The Moderator of the Free Church Federal Council attended a large boy scout camp one baking-hot summer day attired in his full robes. An Anglican bishop was due to lead a short service but there wasn't any sign of him. As the dignitaries waited under the blazing sun, the Moderator, who was becoming increasingly uncomfortable from his dog collar downwards, turned to one of the other clergymen and asked crossly, 'When's this damned bishop going to turn up?' An elderly scout standing nearby, attired in shorts, shirt and scout tie, coughed awkwardly and said, 'Actually, I'm already here.'

A Free Church minister who enjoyed a warmer relationship with his Church of England parish priest once agreed to take a service for him. His friend also asked him to wear a surplice to maintain some continuity for the congregation. When they met again he asked how things had gone, to which his Free Church friend replied, 'Fine, fine. But I was damned glad to get my trousers back on again afterwards.'

Further innocent misunderstandings can be caused by the difference between various Anglican clergy. For example, a visitor to the home of a country parson was very taken by the house and asked enthusiastically, 'Now tell me, is this a wreckage, or a victory?'

At the end of the day the differences between faiths are frequently more in the eyes of the beholder than those who practise them, as a preacher one lunchtime at Lincoln's Inn Fields told his listeners, 'I am a Jew; you are Christians. The only difference between us is that I don't go to synagogue on Saturday and you don't go to church on Sunday.'

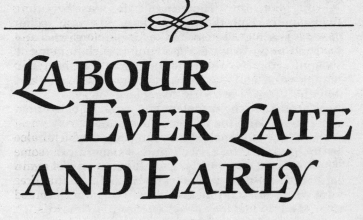

LABOUR EVER LATE AND EARLY

When the *News Chronicle* was describing a devout Anglican many years ago, it said of his faith, 'His religion, deeply felt, is that English one which through the assured centuries has tamed a storm on Galilee to the formal loveliness of a lily-pond in an Essex garden', and it is that image of tranquil serenity, where nothing ever happens, and change, such as it is, comes and goes imperceptibly, that the Church is trying to replace today with one more attuned to the turbulent waters of contemporary society – at least it is in some quarters.

There's the story about the young curate who hurries up to his vicar in church and whispers excitedly, 'There's an old man in a long white beard sitting at the back of the church who says he's God! What do you want me to do?' 'Go and keep and eye on him,' said the vicar, 'and try and look busy!' In the eyes of many laity that's how the Church has always seemed to operate.

Church people know that's certainly not the case today in the majority of parishes, and they also know that many of the problems that seem most pressing today have really been with us for centuries. Take the problem of money. Dear Queen Anne may have set up the Church comfortably with her Bounty nearly three hundred years ago, but her generosity then has been causing its problems ever since, with Anglicans getting increasingly huffy about shelling out more and more of their own money to pay for the Church in its widest sense. Faced with this reluctance clergy have adopted some inspired methods of collecting offerings.

The first vicar of St John's, Red Lion Square, in London, which was bombed during the Second World War, developed the forthright habit of standing up in buses to tell his fellow passengers: 'Ladies and gentlemen. I am building a beautiful church in the slums. I am sure you would like to help me with this work. If you will kindly give me your names and addresses, you will hear from me later' – at which point he produced a notebook and pencil and solemnly made his way through the bus, on both decks.

Less than a century after Queen Anne, a West Country clergyman feeling the pinch made regular trips to Bath to meet the well-to-do patients taking the waters there, to whom he would suggest: 'If God has granted you a cure, you could not show your gratitude better than by helping me in my work; and if by chance the cure has been withheld no doubt you will remember me in your will.'

Similar resourcefulness was shown by the clergyman towards the end of the last century who, appealing for funds to rebuild his church, wrote to the distinguished politician, John Bright. Bright, who had been a strong supporter of the move to disestablish the Irish Church, replied that he regretted he could not help, explaining that it was against his long-held principles to help in building churches associated with the Established Church. By return of post the vicar replied to reassure Bright that, as the ancient building which it had become necessary to replace was still standing, he could still make a valuable contribution – towards its demolition.

Bishops, too, are faced with the pressing need to raise funds. Samuel Wilberforce encountered a wealthy, but tight-fisted, financier who showed more than usual reluctance to contribute to diocesan funds. After several appeals the old skinflint reluctantly agreed and told the bishop, 'I shall be happy to give my mite.' 'I always thought that there were two,' replied Wilberforce, 'and that they represented the widow's all.'

Many wealthy benefactors leave making their contributions until the last minute, like the rich man who received some criticism for spending an excessive amount of money on building a large, impressive church. In his defence he said that he'd owed his success to always having an eye to the future, 'and now I remember I have the Jordan to cross, and if my luggage is too heavy I may sink, so I decided to off-load some of my cargo on that bank on which it is likely to bring the best return.'

Boosting collections in church is itself an art. Jonathan Swift found a successful formula which he used when preaching sermons for charity. During his address he made no mention of the charity at all. Only at the end did he tell the congregation that there was a matter of business to attend to, and then spoke briefly about it in the manner of 'This Week's Good Cause'. After explaining in a matter-of-fact way that there were poor people who looked to them for help, he read the text 'He that giveth to the poor, lendeth to the Lord', and added, 'if you approve of your security, down with your money,' and signalled to the sidesmen to take round the collecting plates.

A preacher in Wales adopted a more subtle, but just as successful, approach when taking a service in a parish which had become notorious for sheep-stealing. Before the collection was made, he stressed the gravity of offering ill-gotten gains at the Lord's altar and expressed his hope that no one involved in sheep-stealing would make a contribution in his presence. When the collection was made not a single man or woman present failed to contribute something!

By complete accident, another preacher also inspired a brimming collection plate when a note was handed to him during a service asking whether there would be any objection to a bankrupt making an offering to the Lord. He told the congregation that he felt certain God saw no bar to bankrupts contributing to His cause, and when the collection was counted in the vestry after the service it revealed that the solvency of that congregation surpassed that of any other to which he had preached.

George Whitefield, one of the founders of Methodism, preferred the direct approach and announced to one of his congregations, 'We will now sing a hymn, which will be followed by the collection. This will give those who do not choose to give their mite a chance to sneak off.' Again, no one moved.

Preachers with less presence can't hope to be as successful, and their disappointment has been expressed in comments like that of the vicar, recently arrived in a parish, who said in church one Sunday, 'I have tried to reach the poor of this parish and I can only conclude from the size of last week's collection, that they have come.'

I like the explanation put forward by the vicar who suggested that a slight error in vocabulary might have been responsible for a meagre collection during one of his services. 'When I explained to you last week that philanthropy was the love of our species,' he said, 'you must have understood me to say "specie" [coined money], which may account for the smallness of the collection. I hope you will prove today that you no longer labour under the same mistake.'

When the traditional substitute for coins of the realm disappeared from one collection plate, another vicar wrote in the parish magazine: 'The absence of buttons from church collections is not due to the realization that it is sinful to pretend ... but to the fact that buttons are costlier than coppers nowadays.'

If buttons won't do, congregations think up other ways of keeping their money from the Lord. One tight-fisted woman who attended church twice a day every Sunday used to avoid the offertory bag altogether by telling the sidesman at matins, with a smile, 'I am coming this evening,' and telling the one taking the collection at evensong, again with a smile, 'I was here this morning.'

Or there was the visitor to a church service at which the sermon had been preached on the importance of missionary work in distant lands and where the collection was going to be given towards this work. However, when the collecting plate arrived at his pew,

'Would you care to say grace.'

this fellow told the churchwarden, 'It's a principle of mine never to give to missions.' 'In that case, help yourself,' said the warden, thrusting the plate at him, 'we're collecting for the heathen tonight!'

Spreading the Gospel in far-off lands can be a costly exercise, admittedly. There used to be a high rate of turnover among missionaries for one thing; there was the story of the priest who was asked whether a colleague had been a successful missionary, and who replied with disturbing honesty, 'Yes, he certainly was. He gave the tribesman they sent him to their first taste of Christianity.' Or there was the case of the rugby international, a native of the Pacific, who became one of the most talented players of this century. He was interviewed after a match in which he had given an outstanding performance and was asked whether his natural instinct for the game was due to having rugby in his blood. He said that it most likely was, and went on to explain, 'My grandfather, who lived on our island when it was still cannibal, once ate a large portion of a missionary who had been a Cambridge blue.'

Missionary work was expensive in equipment too. The records of one missionary society suggested the following as a suitable wardrobe for those it sent overseas: fine calico shirts (48), nightshirts (18), lawn handkerchiefs (18), nightcaps (18), neck-handkerchiefs (24), fine cotton hose (24 pairs), black silk half-hose (2 pairs), black satin waistcoats (4), camblet waistcoats (2), black leghorn hat (1).

The value of their work depended largely on the pastoral gifts of the individual, and those who had to communicate in obscure languages had an added difficulty, typified perhaps by the missionary who valiantly tried to translate key passages of the Prayer Book into the little-known dialect spoken by his flock, but made a slip with the benedictory line, 'Lord dismiss us with Thy blessing', which reached his listeners as, 'Lord, kick us out softly.'

In those countries or cities where missions for different denominations proliferated, the inhabitants seldom appreciated the finer doctrinal distinctions that separated them and opted for more obvious classifications. In Peking, for instance, there used to be a Baptist centre which practised total immersion;

another where sprinkling was permitted; and a Quaker meeting house where no form of Baptism was administered. These became known as 'The Big Wash Faith Hall', 'The Little Wash Faith Hall', and 'The No-Wash-at-all Faith Hall'.

Even among Christians from different European countries innocent mix-ups can occur in what is considered to be acceptable. An Anglican bishop, holidaying with his wife in Andalusia, completed the registration form in their first hotel, filling in their names as he always did: The Bishop of Truro (or wherever it was) and Mrs Jones. As the porter was carrying their cases to the lift, the hotel manager hastened from his office holding the completed form and, taking the bishop to one side, pointed to the two names and said, 'In Spain, Your Grace, we do not let such things be known.'

No doubt he dealt with that situation with the 'tranquil serenity' mentioned earlier, much as a vicar did when he was also placed in an awkward position in a matter concerning his wife. He was attending a large ecclesiastical gathering in which a number of fringe meetings had generated a good deal of violent disagreement and ill-will. At one of these he was openly accused of having violently dragged his wife from an earlier meeting attended by his opponents and compelling her against her will to return to their hotel with him. He listened to the accusation without interruption and when invited to say what he could in his defence, told the meeting, 'In the first place I never attempted to influence my wife in her views, nor her choice of a meeting. Secondly, my wife was not present at the meeting in question. In the third place, I did not attend the meeting myself. To conclude, neither my wife nor myself had any inclination to go to the meeting. Finally, I never had a wife.'

The same sang-froid was called for by the country parson cycling round his parish one night a few years before the Great War who came across a motorist whose car headlights had failed. These were of the pre-dynamo type that operated on acetylene gas, and the vicar, having some vague belief that adding water might help, cheerfully unzipped his flies to pee into the lamp, saying, 'Since there's no water about, we'll have to make do with that with which the Good Lord has provided us.' He could only manage one lamp, however, and told the driver, 'I'm afraid that's all I've got. You'll have to have a go now.' 'I'd love to,' replied the motorist, removing her hat and goggles, 'but I'm afraid the Good Lord forgot to make adequate provision in my case.'

The blushes were on the other cheek half a century later when this amusing episode in the life of another parish priest took place. Annoyed that no one answered his knocking when he had made a special visit and could hear music playing inside the house, a vicar left his visiting card, having written on the back, 'Revelations, 3.10' ('Behold, I stand at the door, and knock: if any man hear my voice, and open the door, I will come in to him ...'). As the congregation were filing out after matins the next Sunday, one of his lady parishioners handed him an envelope and hurried away. Inside he found a card on which was written, 'Genesis, 3.10' ('I heard thy voice in the garden, and I was afraid, because I was naked; and I hid myself ...').

The Church has always maintained a sense of chivalry towards women, which can't make the current wrangling over the ordination of women priests any easier. Dean Inge used to say that he could never forgive Hamlet for 'his caddish behaviour towards Ophelia'. And the reply of the bishop asked by a lady visitor about religious art was also typically gallant. She was curious to know why so many angels depicted in paintings and statues appeared as either women, or young men without beards or moustaches. In reply the bishop told her, 'Everyone knows that women naturally inherit the Kingdom of Heaven, but the men only get in by a very close shave.'

The Church has been careful to exercise great tact as well, even to the extent of modifying its liturgy. A preacher who delivered a sermon under the title 'Ecology - the Rape of the Earth' must have felt gratified that the second collect read at morning service was omitted, thus removing the potentially awkward phrase, 'thou art the author of peace and lover of concord...'

Sometimes this sensibility can be taken too far, as in the case of a very refined clergyman who referred in his sermon to 'Jonah's painful plight in the whale's... er... society.'

A fellow member of the cloth, clearly cast in the same mould, was invited to attend a public meeting for which he prepared what he considered to be an erudite speech. To his disgust, however, he found that the purpose of his invitation had merely been to say a prayer before the meeting began. And in order to give voice to his oratory, he managed to incorporate most of what he had planned to say in his prayer, even to the extent of saying at one point, 'in case that last point should appear too obscure, O Lord, permit Thy servant to illustrate it with this anecdote...'

It's attitudes like these that have led to some of the alarming examples of 'churchese' that have appeared in print. A book written to advance the cause of Church reform contained the passage:

> Whether we think of the fruits of such experience as the nourishment of our own spirits in days in which nourishment is hard to come by from our immediate surroundings, or as a means by which we may find entry into the lives of others and as a store from which we may enrich them, we should find it hard to regard it as a mere decorative addition to, a mere embellishment of, our mutual calling.

While another on missions offered this nugget of wisdom:

> A new vision of God and of His purpose for the world is to quicken a world-wide fellowship to an intensity of service and partnership and a new efficiency in the service of mankind.

So it's no wonder that one of the old school of bishops, who had little truck with the trend he saw in modern Anglicanism to equate the temporal too literally with the spiritual, passed this comment on a recently published devotional manual: 'I suppose it's full of sentences like "For the Greater Duck-billed Platypus we thank Thee, O Lord"!'

Efforts to bring the liturgy more into line with modern life have met with criticism from the laity too. A vicar preaching in Sussex thirty odd years ago decided to offer his own 'modernized' version of the Ten Commandments, the fourth of which ran as follows, 'Remember that thou goest easy in the evil necessity of work. Five days mayest thou labour with every possible rest for tea. On the sixth day or the seventh thou mayest do overtime, double rates, for this is the law of the union. On the seventh day thou canst please thyself about bed or sport and read the Sunday newspapers.' Trades unionists preferred the version Moses brought down from Mt Sinai and complained to the Bishop of Chichester.

A vicar in the same diocese decided forty years ago that it was time the work of the Church extended to the motoring public, and in an effort to cut down motor accidents he invited drivers to bring their cars to church on Rogation Sunday to be blessed; though the press report of this novel event warned: 'Drivers who do not observe the simple rule of the road will in no way benefit from this benediction.'

Services held for motor cars can remain more or less under the vicar's control; the same can't be said, though, of the services that are sometimes held by well-meaning parsons for pets and other domestic animals. At one of these, held to commemorate the feast day of St Francis, the congregation, which included rabbits, guinea-pigs, cats, dogs, two goats, a donkey and a goldfish in its bowl, were being led in their morning prayer when a late arrival on her pony hurried into the church and dismounted in the nave as the vicar began the general Confession, 'Almighty and most merciful father...' But while the pony's rider found her place in the prayer book and joined in, the pony was moving about most uncomfortably. 'We have left undone those things which we ought to have done,' recited the congregation, 'And we have done those things which we ought not to have done,' at which point the pony gave up its internal struggle and did just that.

Having animals in church was one of the many unusual features of the ministry of the Reverend Robert Hawker, for forty years vicar of Morwenstow in Cornwall, who wrote 'Song of the Western Men' and 'And shall Trelawney die?' Hawker was usually followed to church by nine or ten of his own cats who clambered over him, the pews, pulpit and congregation during the service, although one that caught and killed a mouse during a service was excommunicated and forbidden to enter the church again. To a parishioner who tried to shoo a dog out during his sermon, Hawker said, 'Let him be, there were dogs in the Ark, remember.' And when his old clothes were finally discarded and given to a scarecrow, the birds recognized their long-time friend and flocked to his side for a handful of crumbs, as they had grown used to doing. The farmer was more careful about where he sought his scarecrow's wardrobe after that.

If the crows recognized Hawker's attire, they weren't alone. Like many aspects of his mission, the way he dressed was at some divergence to that of his fellow clergy. In his opinion the black normally worn by clerics made him look like 'a waiter out of place or an unemployed undertaker', so he created his own outfit that consisted of a brown cassock adorned with velvet cuffs and topped with a black velvet hat. On high days and holidays he would sport more colourful garments that included a three-quarter-length purple coat, yellow poncho and scarlet gauntlets, in various imaginative combinations. His wife's funeral was marked by the wearing of a pink fez.

He also adopted a practical approach to his pastoral work, removing the panelling from the pulpit to allow the congregation the dubious advantage of seeing the priest's feet. And when repairs were due to the church roof, Hawker instructed the builder to use wood rather than slate; less efficient at keeping out the rain, he readily acknowledged, but a fitting symbol that the Lord accepted both good and bad 'materials' in His house.

Further to the south in the same county the people of the parish of Warleggan, near Bodmin Moor, were saddled with an incumbent of a less gregarious nature, the Reverend F.W. Densham, who was finally called to give an account of his actions before his Maker in 1953. By that time attendance at his church had dropped to nil. As parishioners fell by the wayside, Densham replaced them with cut-out figures or name cards, to which he administered every Sunday. As rector he was not an easily approached man and became even less accessible after erecting an eight-foot barbed-wire fence round the rectory. And his redecoration of the twelfth-century parish church in blue and red, with black and white striped pillars did little to endear him to his congregation.

Understanding lies at the heart of all harmonious relationships between a clergyman and his congregation: parishioners expect certain qualities in their parson and learn to recognize them in others. Sometimes things go wrong though, as was the case with the man who, having offered to accommodate a visiting clergyman, waited for his train at the station and scrutinized every man getting off. To his disappointment no dog collar appeared, but seeing a man with the recognizable bearing of a clergyman, he approached and asked, 'Excuse me, but are you the Reverend Thomas?' 'I'm afraid not,' the other replied. 'It's my dyspepsia that makes me look like that.'

The laity also like services and sermons that they can follow without difficulty. A vicar who had been told by his churchwardens that there had been complaints about his sermons, made a special effort the following week and delivered one that was well received by everyone. In the vestry afterwards the wardens congratulated him warmly, though one of them asked, 'Pardon me, Vicar, but after you said the dedication at the start of the sermon and before you gave the ascription at the end, you made the most unusual movements with your hands over your head. Was that deliberate?' 'It certainly was,' said the vicar. 'Those were the quotation marks.'

Visits by clergymen to hospitals don't always have the comforting effect they intend. A Free Church minister doing his rounds of a geriatric ward, talking to the patients and jotting down any requests they had, went over to the bed of one old lady, who shooed him away nervously, saying, 'Don't come to me, I'm insured with the Co-op.'

Seen from the other side there can't have been much cheer for the vicar, himself lying in a hospital bed, who was visited by a churchwarden bearing the glad tidings, 'Vicar, we had a PCC meeting last night and a resolution put forward wishing you a speedy recovery was carried by eight votes to seven.'

Maybe it was during his absence that his stand-in, addressing the congregation for the last time, tried to draw an analogy between his role and the church fabric that he thought they would understand. The church stood in a run-down area, where vandalism was high. Many of the windows in the church itself were broken and filled with plywood, to which the preacher made reference, saying, 'Much as I have enjoyed being with you, I am not your vicar; rather like those pieces of wood in the windows, they are not real panes, they are substitutes – I too have been merely a substitute.' When the service was over he stood at the door and said goodbye to the congregation as they left, and one elderly man grasped his hand and said, 'I want you to know, sir, that in this parish we will always remember you as a real pane.'

Parishioners who show an interest in their incumbent's work will meet with some unexpected revelations at times. A vicar who was asked by one of his flock what he thought had been his principal contribution to the life of the church in his first twelve months, replied positively, 'People here didn't know what sin was until I came.'

Also unexpected was the apology made by a vicar who had noted the wrong time in his diary for the annual Harvest Supper and consequently turned up an hour after it had started. Fortunately everyone present was in a jovial mood and in this manner he sought to explain his absence: 'Ladies and gentlemen, I can't remember ever being late for such a function as a Harvest Supper before, but it seems tonight that I have well and truly clotted my botty book...'

In spite of the trials and tribulations that beset the clergy in their work, their relationship with the Lord remains paramount, as indeed it should. As Lord Charteris, a former Provost of Eton, once pointed out, the hallmark of Anglicanism, according to an Arab friend of his, was the good manners invariably shown to the Almighty; borne witness to in the account of the clergyman flying to America. The stewardess had asked whether he wanted a drink and he'd ordered a whisky and soda. While this was being fetched, the pilot's voice came on the Tannoy, telling the passengers that they were moving up to forty thousand feet to find a smoother ride. When the clergyman's drink was brought he accepted the soda but declined the whisky, explaining to the stewardess, 'I'm getting a bit near head office.'

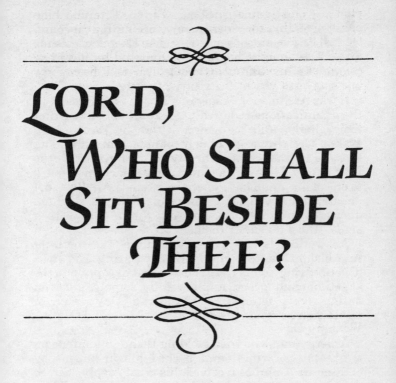

LORD, WHO SHALL SIT BESIDE THEE?

Let's turn our attention now to the Church's hierarchy, a source of amusing speculation for countless generations of Anglicans. 'How can a bishop marry? How can he flirt?' enquired the Reverend Sydney Smith, who pointed out, 'The most he can say is, "I will see you in the vestry after the service."'

It was Archbishop Magee of York who reduced to two the qualifications required to make a bishop: to suffer fools gladly, and to answer letters by return post. Bishop Creighton of London counted himself among those who had great difficulty in conforming to the first. After addressing a particularly trenchant remark to one of his junior clergy, who answered, 'Ah, Bishop, I am afraid that you don't suffer fools gladly,' Creighton answered grandly, 'No, no!' and then added with a smile, 'But I *do* suffer them.'

Answering letters can itself often tax both of Archbishop Magee's criteria. Bishop Baring (known as 'Over-bearing' to his clergy) took great exception to the sanctimonious practice followed by some of them in dating their letters 'St Cuthbert's Day', etc. In retaliation he would head his reply, 'Auckland Castle – Washing Day'.

A clergyman who tried tackling Bishop Blomfield on a question of ritual and backed his argument by quoting St Ambrose received this crusty reply: 'Sir, St Ambrose was not Bishop of London, and I am. Yours truly, W. Lond.'

Bishop Stubbs of Oxford was also an accomplished master of the terse reply. A fussy vicar once wrote a long and detailed letter to him, asking whether in his lordship's opinion he needed to have a faculty in order to install some curtains behind the holy table of his church, to serve as a reredos. Bishop Stubbs replied, giving his views on the subject. The vicar remained unsatisfied and replied with a second letter as long as the first, repeating much of what he had already written on the subject of the reredos. The bishop's reply

to this was shorter: 'Dear Slimeweed [or whatever his name was], Hang your curtains! Yours truly, W. Oxon.'
To a cleric who asked leave of absence for three months to visit the Holy Land, he replied in similar vein: 'Dear Sinecure, Go to Jericho. Yours ever, W. Oxon.'

A rector who once asked Bishop Stubbs to bring his pastoral staff when he came to preach at his church received his lordship's reply, confirming the date of his visit to which he had added below his signature, 'PS - I shall not bring my PS.'

Stubbs had little time for unnecessary ritual either, and he used to tell of the occasion when he attended a service given by a certain Dr Ellis which was a hymn to ecclesiastical ritual in every respect. After one particularly flamboyant function, someone whispered to Stubbs asking what 'use' they were supposed to be following, 'Sarum', 'English', 'Roman', what? 'Ellis in Wonderland, I fancy' Stubbs answered back.

Samuel Wilberforce, one of Stubbs's predecessors in the See of Oxford had little time either for pompous or self-opinionated clergy. Invited once to preach in a village church in deepest rural Oxfordshire, he became exasperated by the vicar's constant reminders to keep his sermon simple. Once in the pulpit he began with the words, 'Around us we see the apotheosis of Nature, apodeictic of theopractic cosmogeny' - and then continued, after a glance at the vicar, to preach a simple and moving Harvest Festival sermon.

At the other end of the scale of intellectual pretensions came Dr Whewell, the famous Master of Trinity, who held a profound contempt for the intelligence of undergraduates, which he never attempted to hide from them. On one occasion he opened a sermon on the Parable of the Talents with the comment, 'In this place, gentlemen, we need only consider the man with one talent.' Little wonder that when Whewell was offered a bishopric and is supposed to have replied, 'There are many bishops, but there is only one Master of Trinity,' the comment was, 'Thank Heavens for that.'

Interviewing a candidate in the university divinity exams during his viva, Dr Merry asked him to translate from the Greek version of the New Testament. The man stumbled and floundered until Merry finally enquired, 'Are you aware that an English translation of this book has been published?'

This reminds me of the story told of Oscar Wilde under the same circumstances. Again asked to translate orally from the Greek New Testament during his viva, Wilde was presented with the account of Christ's Passion. This he rendered into English fluently and accurately, satisfying his examiners after a few sentences that he had more than reached the required standard. The Chairman told him that he need not continue further. Wilde continued translating however, seeming not to have heard him. Again the Chairman told him he could stop, to which Wilde replied, 'Do let me go on. I want to see how it finishes.'

In more recent times, Archbishop Ramsey put his own intellectual prowess to use for a different purpose. Whereas he had occasionally been seen to close his eyes for a moment or two in some of the more tedious debates in the Church Assembly, on one occasion he was spotted writing with concentration to the evident delight of the speaker, who took the opportunity to address many of his comments directly to the Archbishop. After the debate a friend commented on his unusual interest in the proceedings. 'I was writing out the names of all the prime ministers since 1910 in chronological order,' replied the Primate of all England. 'I got them all right except for Asquith.'

It was one prime minister in particular, Lord Palmerston, who hoped to get the better of Bishop Wilberforce during a weekend at his country seat in Hampshire. After lunch it was suggested that everyone should visit some new cottages that Palmerston had built on the estate; some went by carriage, others, Wilberforce among them, chose to walk. A shower of rain fell on the walking party as those in the carriages joined them for the last part of their outing, and Palmerston, looking from his carriage, quoted as he passed the Bishop from Tate and Brady's version of the first Psalm, 'How blest is he who ne'er consents by ill advice to walk.' To which Wilberforce instantly replied, 'Nor sits where men profanely talk.' Touché!

The following reply was sent by the Reverend Charles Inge to a relative, we are told, 'after the receipt of a batch of Limericks of a particularly piquant kind'.

> Your verses, dear Fred, I surmise,
> Were not meant for clerical eyes.
> The Bishop and Dean
> Cannot think what they mean,
> And the curate turns pink with surprise.

There are many examples of the ready wit that made Wilberforce the most celebrated clergyman of his day. Challenged once to find a rhyme for Timbuctoo, he took only a moment's hesitation to compose the verse:

> If I were a Cassowary
> On the plains of Timbuctoo,
> I would eat a missionary,
> Coat and bands and hymn book too.

His sermons were frequently printed in newspapers almost verbatim, and one story tells of the time when two young men were reading one of these in a railway carriage when the train stopped at a station and to their surprise the Bishop of Oxford himself joined and took the seat opposite. 'That's Soapy Sam,' whispered one of the young men. 'Tell him you've been reading his sermon and ask him to tell you the way to Heaven.' His friend complied and in answer to the question Wilberforce replied urbanely, 'The best way to Heaven? Why, turn to the right and keep straight on.'

Getting the better of Wilberforce, then, was no mean triumph and the author of one of the most famous verbal victories was the Reverend Frank Burges, rector of Winterbourne, Bristol, and formerly a fellow of St John's. Burges was a clergyman of the old school and rode to hounds with all the enjoyment of R.S. Surtees, a pastime for which Wilberforce had occasion to take him to task. Burges said in his defence that he didn't think hunting less worthy of a clergyman than dancing. 'I perceive you allude to my being present at the Queen's State Ball at Windsor,' said Wilberforce, 'but I give you my word that I was never in the same room as the dancers.' 'Your Grace,' replied Burges, 'my horse and I are getting old, and we are never in the same fields as the hounds!'

A generation before Wilberforce, the outstanding wit

of the Anglican Church was Sydney Smith, Canon of St Paul's. The stories about him have proliferated like those of Oscar Wilde or Dorothy Parker, and in his case, too, humour and intelligence still manage to shine through. Seeing a child stroking a tortoise he commented. 'This is like scratching the dome of St Paul's to please the Dean and Chapter.' When a man whom he had just outwitted in an argument told him, 'If I had a son who was an idiot, I would make him a parson,' he replied. 'Your father was clearly of a different opinion.' Paying a call on a fellow writer in Edinburgh he found the man earnestly wading through a book he was supposed to be reviewing. Sydney Smith asked him what he was doing, to which his friend enquired how else could he perform his critical task. 'I never read a book before reviewing it,' Smith replied. 'It prejudices a man so.'

He went to Brighton once to lose weight by taking special baths and not-taking his usual delight in the pleasures of the table. A friend who visited him there after a couple of weeks was struck by the success of this therapy and told Smith that he was considerably thinner than when they had last met. 'Yes, I've been here a fortnight,' said Smith, 'and they have scraped enough off me already to make a curate.'

To a friend who asked him later to look back, he confessed: 'My whole life has passed like a razor – in hot water, or a scrape.'

The first time he saw the Prince Regent's recently completed Royal Pavilion at Brighton, he remarked scornfully that it looked as if St Paul's had gone to the sea and pupped.

And when it came to commenting on the Church his own experience lent his remarks a special piquancy. He once drew a famous comparison between a sloth and the Church of England, saying, 'What is most extraordinary is that he lives not upon the branches but underneath them. He moves suspended, and passes his life in suspense – like a young clergyman distantly related to a bishop.'

A worthy successor to Sydney Smith from more recent times was the former Bishop of Durham, Hensley Henson. As chairman of the committee working on the Revised Prayer Book he once got the better of the modernist Bishop of Birmingham, Dr Barnes. Arriving late for one of their meetings, Barnes was unable to find a chair which allowed Henson to greet him saying, 'There you are, Barnes, at last, but I can't see a chair for you. Well, the only thing you can do is anticipate the inevitable decision of the Church, and sit on the fire.'

Henson paid a visit to Cosmo Gordon Laing, shortly after the Archbishop had had his portrait painted. He was keen to hear what Henson thought of it and after allowing him to study it in silence for a moment or two, said, 'I fear it portrays me as proud, arrogant and wordly.' 'To which of the three does your grace take exception?' asked Henson.

Archbishop Frederick Temple was able to deliver as satisfying a riposte to a peer of the realm whose own estimate of his importance tended to exceed that of others. On entering Temple's study he found him seated at his desk and writing, and without looking up the Archbishop invited him to take a chair. 'I don't think you realize who you are addressing,' he answered loftily. Temple stopped writing, looked up and said, 'Very well. Take two chairs.'

He didn't stand any nonsense from the lower orders either. After taking a cab to Fulham Palace he paid the driver the exact fare of one and sixpence to the man's evident disappointment. 'If St Paul were here, he'd have given me more,' he complained. 'If he were here,' said the Bishop of London, 'he'd be Archbishop of Canterbury, live at Lambeth, and the fare is one shilling.'

Before coming to London, Temple had been bishop of

Exeter, where, soon after his appointment, he was walking through the city and spotted the placard for the evening paper that read, 'Astounding statement by the new bishop of Exeter.' Wondering which of his statements had been singled out, he bought a copy and read by the light of a street lamp, 'The new Bishop of Exeter presided this afternoon at the annual meeting of the Church of England Temperance Society, and made the astounding statement that he had never been drunk in his life.'

Temple was once characterized as being like 'granite on fire', a description which aptly reflected his laconic manner of speech. He had little time for embellishment of any sort. To a priest who was performing a number of elaborate genuflections during Holy Communion, he snapped, 'Mr Vicar, don't fidget.' Another, who told him that a particular ritual was customary in his church, was told, 'Well, it won't be customary today.'

He preferred moderation in the speech of others too. To a chatty young priest riding in the same coach as himself and an archdeacon, Temple remarked, 'If you must talk, talk to the archdeacon.'

'I'm not made of sugar,' was his reply to a thoughtful curate who offered him an umbrella once to go home with on a wet night.

A vicar who asked his advice on whether or not to accept a bishopric was asked, 'Why not?' 'Well, your lordship, I am no preacher,' said the man humbly. 'I know that,' said Temple. 'I have heard you twice.'

Another who was anxious about accepting a similar appointment was asked, 'Why should you not accept it?' 'Because I realize the work is so arduous that it would kill me inside a year.' 'Well, what of that?' scoffed the bishop. 'Do your duty.'

The See of Exeter was also held by the kindly but very absent-minded bishop, Lord William Cecil, who ranks among that gentle band of eccentrics who give the Church of England a unique appeal. His lordship was a keen cyclist and left his palace one hot day for a ride in the country. Two miles outside Exeter he realized that the bicycle he was riding didn't belong to him, so he turned round and cycled back to find his own. By the time he was back in the city, however, he'd forgotten why he'd returned and set out once more for the open road, still riding the wrong bicycle.

From the other end of the country, and from an earlier era, comes a matching story told of Dr John Duncan of New College, Edinburgh. He was once invited to preach in a country church outside Aberdeen, where he happened to be staying, and on the appointed Sunday left the city by pony. A brisk wind was blowing that day and when he stopped to take a pinch of snuff, Dr Duncan turned the pony round, so his back was to the wind and the snuff didn't blow away. This task completed, he pocketed his snuff box, touched the pony's sides and set it forward at a trot, which soon brought him back to Aberdeen!

A further example of his amiable but dotty nature was the occasion when he stepped into an Edinburgh street and collided with a passing cow. Raising his hat, Duncan stuttered, 'I beg your pardon, madam,' and hurried on his way.

Archbishop Trench of Dublin had a bizarre encounter with a real-life lady, which has passed into the annals of Church folklore. As old age approached, Trench became obsessed by the fear of sudden and crippling paralysis. One evening he was invited out to dine and throughout dinner was heard muttering to himself, 'Come at last; so it's come at last - total insensibility in the right limb.' As coffee was brought, the lady beside him turned and said, 'Your Grace, it may be of some comfort and relief to you to know that during the whole of the meal it has been my leg that you have been pinching.'

Two centuries earlier Bishop Burnett had counted among the leading churchmen of the day, though he too suffered from moments of forgetfulness as he grew older. He was dining with Sarah, the first Duchess of Marlborough, some time after her husband's fall from favour with Queen Anne, brought about in no small measure by his wife's irascible nature. When the conversation settled on the Duke, Burnett drew a comparison between him and the famous Byzantine general, Belisarius. How was it, enquired the Duchess, that so great a man could find himself rejected and estranged from those who he had served so faithfully? 'Why, madam, he had a brimstone of a wife,' explained Burnett.

In this century no one in the Church of England can hold a candle to the Reverend Archibald Spooner when it comes to eccentricity. It's questionable how many spoonerisms were genuinely of his making, but like Mrs Malaprop he has become affectionately rooted in the language, so does it really matter whether or not he stood up in New College Chapel and announced the first line of John Chandler's hymn as 'Kinquering Congs their titles take'; whether he sent down an undergraduate with the words, 'You have deliberately tasted two worms and you can leave Oxford by the town drain'; or whether, again in the college chapel, he told a visitor, 'Excuse me, but you are occupying my pie,' to which the man replied with commendable presence of mind, 'I do apologize, but I am afraid I was sewn into this sheet'? The fact is that according to all who knew him, these were the very things he might have said.

Spooner's command of English was genuinely maverick. 'You will find as you grow older,' he is on record as confiding, 'that the weight of rages will press harder and harder on the employer.' Meeting a man who had gone down from New College several years earlier, he was greeted with, 'Good evening, Dr Spooner. I doubt if you remember me. My name is...' 'On the contrary,' cut in the Warden, 'I remember your name perfectly, but I must admit that I have completely forgotten your face.' And, speaking of a widow of his acquaintance, he said, 'Poor soul, very sad; her late husband, you know, a very sad death – eaten by missionaries – poor soul!'

Another Oxford cleric from Spooner's era, Bishop Charles Gore, had his own brand of earthy eccentricity. To an ultra-pious vicar at whose church he had arrived to preach, Gore enquired cheerfully, 'Can you lend me a Bible? I remembered my pipe, but I've come away without my Bible.'

And Bishop John Wordsworth of Salisbury, Spooner's senior by a year, ensured his own reputation as a leading Church eccentric with behaviour like that witnessed by one of his curates, who stopped the bishop for a brief conversation and was asked by him when it had ended, 'Could you tell me in which direction I was walking when I met you?' 'You were coming down the street, Your Grace.' 'Was I? Well, in that case I must have taken luncheon.'

Bishop Wilberforce used to enjoy telling the story of a parson who took a far greater interest in the delights of the table. If he found it laid for a sumptuous meal, he would begin his grace by saying, 'O most bountiful Jehovah.' If, on the other hand, the selection of cutlery and glass promised less tempting fare, he would say, 'We are not worthy, Lord, of these, the least of Thy mercies.'

Dr Mervyn Stockwood once drew an amusing distinction between High Church and Low Church parishes on the basis of their catering. He had to confess a partiality for High Church ones on the grounds that when staying among Low Church people there was a tendency to be sent to bed with a cup of weak cocoa, which wasn't his idea of a nightcap.

From a century earlier comes the story of the domestic servants preparing for the arrival of a Church dignitary for dinner. The butler was absent as the table was laid and the menu prepared, but he'd left instructions with one of the maids to find out to which branch of the faith the guest belonged. Why was this, asked one of the other servants? 'Because John says, be sure to find out if he is High or Low Church, because High means lots of wine-glasses and Low means plenty of puddings,' the maid explained.

The first time that I was asked to preach myself was by Cuthbert Barsley, then Bishop of Coventry. It was at a call to mission and after I had finished my frightfully bedraggled sermon, I retired trembling to the ecclesiastical equivalent of the green room. The Bishop turned to me and said, 'Well, Derek, it was a wonderful night tonight, God was with us tonight.' I said, 'th... th... th... thank you very much indeed B... B... B... Bishop.' 'Come on,' he said, 'Let's go back to my house and have a drink.' All night I had been longing for a large gin and tonic, and I could practically hear the ice tinkling in a long cool glass as we drove in his car. When we got to the doorway he turned to me again and said, 'Well, Derek, what will you have to drink? Ovaltine, or cocoa?'!

A meal is said to have been the only occasion at which Bishop Woods of Winchester ever made a joke. He was attending a lunch party given on board a yacht during Cowes week and was asked to say grace. Glancing through a porthole before he spoke, he saw rough weather blowing up and said, 'For what we may be permitted to retain, may the Lord make us truly grateful.'

Canon Alfred Ainger, Master of the Temple, produced a timely comment at dinner after accidentally spilling some gravy on the tablecloth. Turning to his hostess, he apologized, 'It ill becomes me to show such disrespect to the cloth.'

A similar mishap originated one of Archbishop Magee's best-known remarks. A waiter spilt hot soup down his neck and with the mildness and serenity that made him famous he asked, 'Is there any layman present who will kindly express my feelings?'

Magee has also gone down in history for the comment he made during a debate in the House of Lords on the Intoxicating Liquor Bill of 1872: 'It would be better that England should be free than that England should be compulsorily sober.' Which explains the disappointment he must have felt when staying with a wealthy host who served an excellent meal, but apologized that there was nothing on the table to drink but water; though he added that Magee would find a little wine in his bedroom. When the invitation was returned and it was Magee's turn to play host, this incident was not forgotten and as they sat down to eat, Magee said to his guest, 'Though there is only wine on the table, I have arranged that you will find a little filtered water in your room when you retire to rest.'

It was this temperate attitude that obliged a more recent Bishop of Colchester to change the name of his cat from Sherry to Shandy after one of his clergy had suggested that 'Sherry was a little too strong.'

Bishop Stubbs seldom suffered anxieties on this score. The morning after he had attended a most impressive and enjoyable banquet the friend who had sat by him at dinner called to enquire whether he had got home safely. The Bishop looked surprised at this question until realization dawned and he hastily replied, 'Indeed! Thank you... yes. It was only my boots that were tight.'

Sartorial concerns have afflicted other bishops too. It used to be said of Archbishop Whatley of Dublin that he never replaced his archiepiscopal stockings when holes were worn in them, nor did he even attempt to have them darned. Instead, he tried disguising the holes by sticking black tape to his calves. (Yet by the time he died Whatley had given an estimated forty thousand pounds to charity thanks to his care with money. In fact, when Newman took over Whatley's rooms in

'You need a pair of trousers more than you need a steeple.'

Oriel, he found the last of the herrings that his predecessor always cooked for his own breakfast still hanging from a string.)

Bishop Stubbs once forgot his academic hood at an occasion when they were to be worn and borrowed one of the same degree from another university. This was spotted by a sharp-eyed observer, who remarked mischievously, 'The Bishop wears a lie on his back.' 'Not so bad as that,' quipped Stubbs, 'only a falsehood.'

There's an engaging story about Bishop Compton of Ely who inherited a cope that had been introduced by his predecessor. When he put it on for the first time he found in it what looked like a small, pink stole and put this on too since he wanted to continue the previous bishop's tradition. This occasioned some comment after which the 'stole' disappeared from the episcopal

wardrobe, once it had been tactfully pointed out that it
had actually been Bishop Woodford's book-mark.

Problems of identity still plague our bishops, even
those called to the highest office. During his time as
Bishop of St Albans, Dr Robert Runcie expressed his
worries about his purple robes to the *Luton Evening
Post*, which reported, '...he hates them, though his
wife thinks they're sexy. He often says he lives in
mortal fear of being in a car accident while on the way
to an engagement. He said, "If I'm knocked
unconscious people will think I'm a transvestite."'

'The usual?'

Dr Geoffrey Fisher, who of course had preceded Dr Runcie as Primate of All England three decades earlier, addressed himself to other problems in the modern world. Speaking on the nuclear threat, which came of age in the year that he moved to Canterbury, Dr Fisher once said, 'The greatest danger of today is not the hydrogen bomb. At its very worst, all that could do would be to sweep a vast number of persons at one moment from this world into the other, and more vital world, into which, anyhow, they must all pass some time.'

On a visit to New York other temporal concerns confronted him. At a press conference held on his arrival he was asked whether he would be visiting any nightclubs in the city. 'Are there any nightclubs in New York?' he asked, which allowed one newspaper to carry the headline the following morning, 'Archbishop's first words on United States soil: "Are there any nightclubs in New York?"'

A leading churchman who turned his hand to journalism after retirement was Dean Inge, who used to recall with a smile the critical comment that he had ceased to be a pillar of the Church and had become instead two columns in the *Evening Standard*.

And after twenty-five years tenure of office Bishop May was presented with an address by the native members of his diocese in which he was described as an 'indomitable wart-hog', an unparalleled testimony to his courage; the wart-hog never turning tail and running away when attacked.

Perhaps the final word on the bishop's lot should go to Dean Alford, who took a critical look at the consequences of higher preferment and decided:

> I'm glad I'm not a bishop,
> To walk in long black gaiters,
> And have my conduct pulled about
> By democrat dictators.

Glorious Things of Thee are Spoken

When I am in the pulpit,' reflected the Reverend Sydney Smith, 'I have the pleasure of seeing my audience nod approbation while they sleep.' Getting on for two centuries later, few preachers would disagree with him in spirit, I suspect.

For all the pearls cast before swine, preaching does have its compensations, as one vicar indicated when he was asked what he considered to be the greatest consolation of his chosen profession. He thought for a moment and then replied, 'I suppose it's the fact that, in the presence of my wife, my children and any number of members of the public I can, for a limited period of time every Sunday, say whatever I like on any subject without fear of interruption or contradiction.' Though this can be an indulgence that sometimes misfires, as was the case of the vicar, standing in for a colleague, who said to one of the churchwardens in the vestry before the service, 'The congregation's a bit thin this morning. Did you tell them I was going to be preaching?' 'No, I didn't,' he answered, 'but you know how things get out.'

Successful preaching is the fruit of careful planning. As the Reverend Robert Hall once explained to a questioner who asked how many sermons a preacher could prepare in a week, 'If he is a man of prominent ability, one; if he is a man of ordinary ability, two; if he is an ass, six.' This was a sentiment shared by another eminent preacher who was asked how long it took him to prepare a sermon, or any other form of public speaking for that matter, and answered, 'If I am going to speak for a quarter of an hour I should like a week to prepare, if I am to speak for half an hour, three days will do, if I can go on for as long as I like, I am ready now' – a point that was sadly lost on the prolix parson who was asked by an anxious colleague on what he proposed to preach, answered 'The milk of human kindness', and received the tart reply, 'Condensed, I hope.'

Monsignor Ronald Knox, an Anglican chaplain before his reception into the Roman Catholic church, was brother to E.V. Knox (*Punch*'s 'Evoe') who wrote this limerick. Perhaps it was a family story?

There was a young curate of Hants,
Who suddenly took off his pants.
When asked why he did,
He replied, 'To get rid
Of this regular army of ants!'

The story is told of a minor canon at Windsor who was suddenly called on at the last minute to preach in St George's Chapel in the presence of Queen Victoria and a number of distinguished guests staying at the castle. In the couple of hours before the service was due to start, the poor man tried to compose something appropriate. During his deliberations he met Benjamin Disraeli taking a stroll after breakfast and sought his advice on what he should preach about. 'About ten minutes,' the prime minister told him.

That advice might have been put to good effect in the case of the Reverend Mr Houston, a Presbyterian minister who was also summoned at short notice to officiate at the kirk at Crathie during one of the good queen's sojourns at Balmoral. Quite overcome by the occasion he reached his highest flights of oratory in a prayer for the Queen herself, in which he entreated the Lord, 'Grant that as she grows to be an old woman, she may be made a new man, and stand before Thee as a pure virgin, bringing forth sons and daughters to Thy glory; and that in all peaceful causes she may go forth before her people like a he-goat on the mountains.' The Reverend Houston was not invited to officiate at Crathie again.

They say that parsons can buy sermons by the bookful. Bishop Doane of Albany was one-time rector of Hartford and at this church Mark Twain was an occasional attender. Twain one Sunday had some fun with the rector – 'Dr Doane,' he said at the end of the service. 'I enjoyed your service this morning. I welcomed it like an old friend. I have, you know, a book at home, containing every word of it.' 'You have not,' said the rector indignantly. 'I have so,' said Twain. 'Well, show me that book, I would like to see it.' The next day Twain sent round to the rector an unabridged dictionary.

A happier fate awaited a young curate who preached his first and meticulously worked sermon in a small country church. The following Friday one of the churchwardens asked if he would mind taking the service that Sunday as the planned preacher had been taken ill. 'I'm not sure,' said the curate. 'I've only just started preaching, you see, and I've only got one sermon prepared.' 'That doesn't matter,' reassured the churchwarden. 'We can't remember a word you said last week, but everyone enjoyed it.'

Not every priest responds with favour to these last-minute summonses. Dean Bickersteth made the mistake of asking the Reverend William St George Paterson, then priest's vicar at Lichfield, if he would preach at very short notice. The request was agreed to, but not with total rapture. Indeed, as a mark of his displeasure, Paterson selected Psalm 119, the longest in the Prayer Book, as his text, read it from beginning to end, paused briefly to explain that it was customary to repeat a text and then read through all one hundred and seventy-six verses once more. The body of his sermon consisted of a commentary on the entire psalm, verse by verse, and when he stepped from the pulpit three hours later only he and the Dean were left in the cathedral. 'Good afternoon, Mr Dean,' said the preacher tartly as he made his exit. 'I fancy you will not command old Paterson to preach in a hurry again.'

Others seem able to adopt a more relaxed approach, like that of a visiting preacher who climbed into a pulpit at matins and told the congregation, 'I am terribly sorry, but I seem to have come without my notes and so I must rely on what the Lord puts into my mouth. If you come to evensong, however, you will hear something very much better.' Or there was the vicar who announced one morning that his sermon would be shorter than usual, not longer than five minutes – news which was followed immediately by the choir singing the anthem 'It is enough'.

The great Baptist preacher Charles Haddon Spurgeon who used to instruct young ministers in the art, always made the point of telling them, 'When you speak of Heaven let your features be irradiated with a heavenly light. But when you talk about hell – your ordinary face will do.' His attention was more favourably received than that of a fussy old vicar who wanted to keep an overzealous eye on his curate's sermons, and sent him a letter asking on what text he proposed to preach on the following Sunday. The reply he received was 'I Thessalonians, 4.11 ('And that ye study to be quiet, and to do your own business...').

Another curate in a similar predicament told his vicar that he had chosen 'The widow's mite' for his first sermon. 'There are only two widows in this village,' commented the vicar, 'and they both do.'

Bishop Hensley Henson, who had a gift for shedding new light on the scriptures, was once asked to preach to a large and influential women's society that gathered once a year in a cathedral for evensong. As was customary, this was preceeded by a sumptuous tea, and eyeing his congregation with a sardonic eye, Henson read his text, 'All such as be fat upon the earth have eaten and worshipped.'

Physical well-being was less in evidence one bitterly cold winter morning as a vicar shuffled his notes awkwardly in his mittened hands and addressed his shivering congregation with Isaiah's comforting words, 'I am warm, I have seen the fire.'

There was a preacher who opened his sermon in the chapel of an asylum with the rhetorical question, 'Why are we all here?', which was met with an alarmingly lucid reply, 'Because we're not all there.' Which got him off to as shaky a start as the priest preaching in defence of High Church principles, who chose to quote from Ezekiel, 1.18: '... they were so high that they were dreadful.'

While seasoned resignation guided the voice of the vicar who chose to address his flock on the relationship of fact and faith. 'That you are sitting in front of me is a fact,' he told them. 'That I am speaking to you from the pulpit is fact. But it is only faith that makes me believe that any of you are listening.'

For any who might have been listening to the stand-in preacher one evening in the University Church in Cambridge, who took the place of the absent Archbishop Magee, the selected passage was unexpectedly apt, 'In Dr Magee's absence,' began the preacher, 'he has asked me to read the sermon he intended to preach. The text is from St Matthew, chapter eleven, verse three, "... Art thou he that should come, or do we look for another?"'

Whereas a fellow bishop who was able to attend a

service in one of the churches in his diocese warmly thanked the congregation for inviting him to preach to them, only to be greeted, as he made his way to the pulpit, by the singing of 'Dear Lord and father of mankind, forgive our foolish ways.'

But it was Archbishop Temple who offered one of the most damning opinions when he went to a church where a young curate was preaching. After the service had finished they left the church together and, trying to discover what Temple had thought of his sermon, the young man commented, 'It was not a bad text I chose, my Lord.' 'I was not finding fault with the text,' grunted the archbishop.

Revenge came to another curate in a similar predicament. He had suffered for over two years with a rather pompous vicar and when a fresh appointment was confirmed, he delivered his last sermon, beginning with the passage, 'Tarry ye here with the ass while I go yonder.'

Of course the Bible isn't necessarily the only source of inspiration in the pulpit. The present controversy surrounding the beliefs (or their interpretation at least) in some sections of the Anglican Church is only the most recent of a succession of fundamental disagreements stretching all the way back to the Reformation. Half a century ago the 'modern' preacher was satirized in the lines:

> His hearers can't tell you on Sunday
>   beforehand
> If in that day's sermon they'll be Bibled or
>   Koran-ed.
> For though wisdom profane with his creed he
>   may weave in
> He makes it quite clear what he doesn't
>   believe in.

On the other hand there are those who question the direct relevance of much in the scriptures to our modern world. One speaker at a church meeting suggested that the parables of the unjust steward and the labourers in the vineyard were quite unsuitable material for Sunday school teaching 'particularly to children brought up with some knowledge of trade union principles'. Taking a step nearer the current of the times was the notice that informed the congregation, 'At both services in the morning it is intended to preach a series of sermons on the "Seven Deadly Sins", omitting lust.'

Times change, and one wonders how today's congregation might respond to the exhortations of a former country cricketer, F.H. Gillingham of Essex, who after retiring from the crease took his batting to the pulpit and at one memorable service implored the elderly matrons seated in front of him 'to keep their bats straight and get their left toe to the pitch of the ball'.

While it should be the 'matter' and not the 'art' of a sermon that holds those listening, there are undoubtedly those preachers whose sense of delivery is sharper than others. Perhaps one Victorian divine went a stage too far in this respect; after his death a collection of his sermons were found in manuscript carefully inscribed with stage directions like, 'Raise the right hand here' – 'Pause for ten seconds' – 'Sink voice to a whisper' – and in one instance 'Weep here'. But that surely is preferable to the device resorted to by a vicar twenty years ago who tried to stem the steady decline in his congregation by introducing a robot preacher into his services. As the *Guardian* reported, 'It is like a television Dalek and its red eyes flash when it talks.'

Flashing red eyes most likely played some part in the first sermon delivered by an especially shy curate. Normally a temperate man, who never touched a drop of alcohol, he knocked back two large tumblers of sherry to steady his nerves before the service and climbed into the pulpit with mounting confidence. Casting aside the notes he'd been poring over all week, he addressed the congregation in simple, unaffected language, speaking from the heart with earnest conviction. 'How did it go?' he asked the vicar after the service. 'As a first sermon, it was truly a remarkable performance,' comforted the older man. 'However, there are three things I ought to mention: first it was the Philistines and not the Russians whom the Israelites defeated; secondly it was David who slew Goliath and not vice versa; and thirdly you may recall that his chosen weapon was a small pebble and not a bloody great boulder. In every other respect I could find no fault at all.'

A young evangelist in the course of an emotional address exhorted his hearers not to leave without clean hearts, pure hearts, loving hearts and sweet hearts.

Blessed with the same gifts was the preacher who followed the announcement of his text with the words, 'This is a text for all, young and old, rich and poor, learned and unlearned, high and low. For you, old man, with hoary head; and for you, young maiden, with your blooming cheek.'

Though a fiery evangelist addressing a large public meeting and urging his listeners to beware the wrath of God on the Day of Judgement, did have his wits about him after thundering a warning about 'weeping and wailing and gnashing of teeth'. No sooner had he delivered these words than an old woman at the back of the hall stood up and called, 'Sir, what about me? I haven't got any teeth left.' 'Have no fear, madam,' he answered quickly and, maintaining his momentum, 'Teeth will, of course, be provided.'

Or there was the old preacher who used to specialize in addressing groups of men on 'masculine' subjects. His particular strength was tales about the hardships endured by the fighting services, in which he was apt to get a trifle tearful and carried away. Friends who arrived late at a Men's Service of his were greeted by the churchwarden's reassurance, 'It's all right. He's just kissed the dying soldier, so he's good for another half-hour yet.'

Dramatic effects and rhetorical flourishes may certainly add zest to a sermon, but they can also backfire terribly. This was the case with an unnamed bishop who was particularly struck by a sermon delivered by a vicar recently arrived in the diocese. At one point he'd announced, 'The happiest days in my life have been spent in the arms of another man's wife...' There was a pause during which the congregation waited in fascination and horror, before he continued serenely, 'In the arms of my mother.' From then onwards he had them in his hands. The bishop was very taken with this and determined to use it in his next sermon in the cathedral; which he duly did. 'The happiest days of my life have been spent in the arms of another man's wife,' he began confidently. Again the congregation, many times larger in this great church, sat back in astonishment, a response that so pleased the old boy that he completely lost his train of thought and after the pause had strayed beyond its intended length, he stuttered in bewilderment, 'But I can't remember whose.'

There was a flattering degree of attention paid to a more recent bishop when he preached in a newly-constructed church for the first time. This had been fitted out with the latest ecclesiastical mod cons and included a sophisticated and somewhat bewildering public address system. Up in the pulpit the bishop tapped the microphone apprehensively and hearing no noise, bent down and whispered, 'There is something wrong with this microphone.' He was wrong, however, and his words echoed round the church, to which the congregation, keyed up, on their best behaviour, and eager to impress him with their grasp of the ASB service, replied instinctively, 'And also with you.'

Less fortunate was the preacher in a strange church who asked obligingly at the start of his sermon, 'Can

'You don't suppose he's miming to a Billy Graham tape?'

you hear me at the back?' 'Yes, I can hear you fine,' answered a voice, 'but I don't mind changing with somebody who can't.'

Not that there is anything new about a congregation's attention straying in church. During the reign of Charles II, Dr Robert South found himself preaching to the King and other members of the court who were gradually falling asleep one by one. Leaving his sermon for a moment, he singled out one of the principal offenders and called to him, 'My Lord Lauderdale, let me entreat you, rouse yourself; you snore so loud that you will wake His Majesty.'

Frequent were the complaints against long-winded sermons, even if they were expressed in a roundabout way, like this observation made one Sunday morning by an elderly parishioner: 'The new vicar's sermon this morning wasn't up to those of our dear old vicar.' 'Why's that?' asked the churchwarden to whom it was addressed. 'Because the new parson took forty minutes to put me to sleep, whereas the old one could do that in fifteen.'

Short and succinct is the advice offered by those who know and those who listen when it comes to sermons; advice admirably followed by a student of Spurgeon's who was asked by the great man to give an off-the-cuff sermon on Zaccheus. 'First, Zaccheus was a man of small stature; so am I,' he began. 'Second, Zaccheus was very much up a tree; so am I. Third, Zaccheus made haste and came down; so will I' – and immediately sat down. His fellow students called for more, but Spurgeon silenced them, saying, 'No, he could not improve upon that if he had tried ever so much.'

Much the same effect was achieved by an incumbent who had a strong dislike of preaching. The efforts of his PCC and a little arm-twisting from the rural dean got him into the pulpit in the end, but not for long. 'Do any of you know what I am going to say?' he asked. 'No,' replied most of them. 'Neither do I,' he answered and left the pulpit. The next Sunday he was once more persuaded to preach to them, and again he began by asking, 'Do any of you know what I am going to say this time?' Ready for him now, they all answered 'Yes'. 'In that case you don't need me to say it,' he replied and left the pulpit. Back there on the third Sunday he asked the same question and received a confused mixture of 'Yes' and 'No' in their replies. But his reply was ready and before stepping down he told them, 'Well, if those of you who answered "Yes" will tell those who answered "No", there still won't be any need for me to tell them.'

Few preachers seem to encourage verbal responses from their congregations while they are preaching; sometimes for obvious reasons. Bishop Boyd-Carpenter of Ripon was once challenged by an unbeliever in the course of a sermon, when the man called out, 'Do you honestly believe that Jonah was swallowed by the whale?' 'When I get to Heaven I will ask him', answered the bishop. 'And suppose he isn't there?' 'In that case – you will have to ask him yourself.'

Well-intentioned, but no less distracting was the zealot who became so wrapped up in a sermon that he invoked his Maker's name whenever he thought a good point had been made. After tolerating a few of these interruptions the preacher's patience finally evaporated and he said tartly, 'I would be grateful if the member of the congregation who keeps calling out "Praise the Lord" would kindly cease and remember that this is the House of God.'

For Bishop Blomfield the most irritating interruption to any public address was a crying baby, and when one started up during the singing of the hymn that preceded one of his sermons he wasted no time in telling the curate to ask the child's mother to take it outside. There was a very large congregation that day and the aisles were so packed that the message failed to get through, which left Blomfield to deal with the matter himself. 'My sermon tonight,' he began, 'is about good resolutions; but good resolutions are no use at all unless they are what that baby must be – carried out.'

So much for those who preach; what matters is how their words are received – not always favourably it would seem. In the eighteenth century Dr Samuel Parr, widely known as 'the Whig Johnson' was invited by the mayor of Oxford to deliver the Spital sermon in Christ Church Cathedral. As they were leaving together at the end of the service Parr asked his host how he had liked his sermon. 'There were four things in it, Doctor, that I didn't like to hear,' he replied. 'State them, then.' 'Well, to speak frankly, they were the quarters of the church clock, which struck four times before you had finished.'

Perhaps a little more justified was the opinion of a churchwarden cursed with a vicar whose opinion of his own rhetoric compelled him to comment after one service, 'I am a very fortunate man! When I go up into the pulpit I hardly ever know what I am going to talk about but I manage to put my sermons across.' 'Same with us, vicar,' muttered the churchwarden. 'When you come down out of the pulpit we seldom know what you have been talking about.'

Less deserved was the fate of a young curate, who found himself ill-prepared and excruciatingly nervous, in the pulpit of the cathedral taking the place of the bishop. Somehow he stumbled through a sermon and in the vestry afterwards apologized to the vicar's warden. 'Don't worry, you did your best,' he said, before adding ruefully, 'It's those who sent you who should be shot.' Though at least he wasn't fishing for compliments like the preacher who remarked to the rector whose parish he was visiting, 'I hope I didn't weary your flock with the length of my sermon.' 'No,' he was told, 'nor by its depth.'

The same treatment was meted out to the vicar who, having been invited by the Dean of his Diocesan Cathedral to preach a sermon, asked what he had thought of it. 'Well, if you must know, I didn't like it,' replied the dean. Incautiously the vicar asked why. 'Firstly you read it. Secondly you read it badly. And thirdly, in my opinion it wasn't worth reading.'

If that isn't conclusive enough, how about an astringent splash of sarcasm, similar to the one awaiting the vicar who, after also asking how his sermon had been enjoyed, received the answer, 'There was one passage at the end I liked very much.' He asked what it was. 'Your passage from the pulpit to the vestry,' he was told.

The opinion of the laity can frequently be ambivalent. Take for example the meeting between an elderly bishop who paid a visit to St Mary's in Oxford, the University Church, and met an even more elderly verger whom he remembered from his days as an undergraduate. During the exchange of customary greetings the verger told him, 'I have much to be grateful for. You know, Your Grace, I have listened to every sermon preached in this church for fifty years and, thank God, I am still a Christian.'

The power of the spoken word is all that some require in a sermon, even if its meaning quite eludes them. An old woman who never missed a service was asked by her vicar how she'd enjoyed listening to a visiting preacher and, more importantly, whether she had understood what he had said. 'Oh, sir would I had the presumption,' she replied.

There can be backhanded compliments too. A nervous curate saying goodbye to the congregation after preaching his first sermon became more and more convinced that it had been a failure, as one by one they shook hands and said their farewells without once mentioning his preaching. It was only towards the end of the line that he received any crumbs of comfort, from a jolly-looking farmer, who gripped his hand like a vice and said enthusiastically, 'Well done, lad! I didn't get a wink of sleep.'

An indolent vicar of Bray
His roses allowed to decay;
His wife, more alert,
Bought a powerful squirt,
And said to her spouse, 'Let us spray.'

No one should underestimate the challenge faced by
preachers today who have to compete with the hard-
selling, image-packed methods employed by Mammon
and his cronies. This might explain why the current
trend in preaching is towards the direct, plain-talking
approach so different from the style of earlier
preachers, personified by the rector who concluded a
sermon on the differences between Christians with the
plea, 'Let us agree to disagree without being disagree-
able'; and championed by the likes of the seventeenth-
century Dean of Gloucester, Knightly Chetwood, who,
when once preaching to the royal court exhorted
sinners to turn from their wicked ways, threatening

them with damnation in 'a place which he thought it not decent to name in so polite an assembly'.

It has to be said that the preacher and preached to in the Church of England do have a reasonably clear idea of the direction in which their faith should be running, unlike one definition of Calvinism which compressed its doctrine into four lines of delightful ambivalence:

> You can and you can't
> You will and you won't;
> You'll be damned if you do,
> You'll be damned if you don't.

Faced with that, it's understandable why there's a temptation to opt for Jonathan Swift's creed of the Anythingarian.

This confusion was highlighted in the eighteenth century by the Marquis Domenico Caracciolo, who is credited with the observation, 'In England there are sixty different religions, and only one sauce.' A century later it was an Oxford tailor who expressed the religious dimension of this argument in an altogether more English way by hanging in his window a sign that read, 'Our clerical outfits are elegant and inexpensive and proclaim at a glance the views of their wearers,' and who used to say of one particular suit, with scarcely concealed pride, 'With that, sir, you can hold any opinion.'

The Vicar of Bray lives on!

Ye Choirs of New Jerusalem

I f you go to church and like the singing better than the preaching, that's not orthodox,' wrote E.W. Howe; in the case of most Anglican churches it's also very unusual.

Unlike other Christian nations the English don't share a universal facility for singing in public – not to the ears of others, at any rate. The Welsh and the Mediterranean peoples may carry their faith forward on a brimming wave of song, but not so the Englishman in his pew, who rarely ventures to disturb the 'lily pond' of his faith with more than a faint ripple during a hymn, which means that when he does let rip the result is seldom as pleasing as it might have been with a little practice. Some, on the other hand, may practise as much as they like without ever improving.

Archbishop Frederick Temple was a case in point. Ever since his schooldays he had enjoyed community singing and, hiding his dog collar, seldom missed the chance to join in a rousing carol or hymn, even during his five years as Archbishop of Canterbury. During a visit to the Midlands one Advent he passed a church holding its carol service and was lured inside. The pews were packed, but squeezing into one at the back, he opened the hymn book and began singing enthusiastically. Sadly, no more than a couple of verses had passed before the man standing next to him said under his breath, 'Dry up, mister, you're spoiling the show.'

Painful home truths also led to the resignation from the church choir of a man who'd always prided himself on his fine tenor voice – that was until his absence from a couple of choir practices, during which one of his colleagues asked if the organ had been repaired.

The pure treble of a cathedral chorister isn't always matched by his carol-singing contemporaries moving from door to door at Christmas time. One little band taking Christmas cheer to the neighbourhood asked for a penny or twopence after singing 'Away in a Manger' at one door, only to be told, 'Here's a shilling.

Now, go and take yourselves off and do your singing twelve streets away!'

A little boy, with more of an eye for the gift of Christmas than the message, knocked at a door in a street near his home and asked the lady who opened it, 'Can we sing some carols for you, missus?' 'We? I can only see one of you,' she answered. 'No, I've got a friend,' he assured her. 'He's working the other side of the street.'

In Cornwall, I'm told, there used to be choirs that moved around the county, joining congregations and blending their words to their hosts' music and vice versa. This could lead to some peculiar compressions or expansions in hymns, resulting in phrases like, 'Come down Sal. Come down Sal. Come down Salvation from on high', which was one inspired opening. Another lamented, 'My poor Poll. My poor Poll. My poor polluted heart.' The soaring soprano strains of 'Oh for a man. Oh for a man. Oh for a mansion of the skies,' was only surpassed by, 'And in the pie. And in the pie. And in the pious He delights.' The second line of 'Before Jehovah's awful throne' could cause problems too and had frequently to be lengthened to fit a tune, with the result that the choir would sing, 'The nations bow-wow-wow with sacred joy.'

The actual length of certain hymns can have a surprising relevance in itself. Archbishop Temple, in spite of his own shortcomings, greatly admired those who would burst into impromptu singing just for the fun of it. He once commended the cook of the household where he was staying for her joyous rendering of 'Nearer My God to Thee', which he heard as he was going down to breakfast. Flattered, though a little flustered, she thanked him but felt obliged to explain, 'That's the hymn I always boil the eggs to, my Lord. Three verses for soft and five for hard.'

Familiarity seems to be the essence of a successful hymn with an English congregation. Give them a hymn or tune they don't know and the results are most dispiriting. Hymn 7 in the *Ancient and Modern* hymn book was announced at a morning service, where the organist, by way of experiment, chose an unfamiliar tune. The first verse passed almost in silence, with only a few pitiful squeaks and murmurs from the congregation. Before the second verse, the vicar silenced the organist and himself led off in the tune they all knew, singing, 'Dark and cheerless is the morn/Unaccompanied by Thee.'

A choir master trying to inject some life into his sullen band asked them to repeat the hymn, 'Little Drops of Water, Little Grains of Sand', and, giving them the note on the rehearsal piano, said, 'Right, one more time. "Little drops of water" – and for goodness' sake put some spirit into it!'

A vicar whose choir and congregation together were just as lifeless, tried to spur them to greater enthusiasm as they sang 'I Cannot Help But Wonder Where I'm Bound' by dancing in the nave and 'showing them how to put across the message in a bouncy way'. Warming to his encouragement, they launched into the second verse when, with his arms waving frenziedly above his head, the vicar suddenly disappeared through a faulty grille in the floor to come to rest on the pile of coke that fired the heating system.

A grille in another church in Cambridgeshire was the undoing of the officiating clergyman there. The service started with a procession from the vestry, led by the choir. As it passed over part of the grating in the floor, one of the girls caught the heel of her shoe in it and rather than upset the ceremony, left it stuck fast to continue with her right foot bare. One of the tenors following her, saw what had happened and bent down to retrieve it. Finding the shoe well and truly jammed, he picked up the whole grating and continued down the nave. The basses following had seen what had happened and made due allowance in their measured tread; not so the clergyman, who found himself suddenly snatched to the nether regions in mid-verse.

A rural dean visiting one of his clergy during his choir's weekly practice came away saddened by what he had heard. Asked by the vicar what he'd thought of their effort, the dean said that the prophecy of Amos, 8.3 had been fulfilled, 'And the songs of the temple shall be howlings in that day.'

One rector, during Bishop Wilberforce's time, tried to introduce the wonders of Gregorian chant to his village choir, in the mistaken belief that this would please the bishop. When Wilberforce indicated that he didn't think his rural parish was quite the place for this, the man complained, 'But, Your Grace, David sang his psalms to Gregorian melodies.' 'Indeed he did,' replied Wilberforce, 'and I don't wonder Saul cast his javelin at him.'

In our own day the value of this form of ecclesiastical music is still questionable in an English setting. A customer in a record shop who asked one of the assistants, 'Have you got any records of Gregorian chant, please?' received the reply, 'I don't know. Does he sing with a band?'

If this makes us smile, it's important to remember that many popular tunes owe their origin to famous religious melodies. The tune of 'Yes, We Have No Bananas' for instance, is said to be founded on a melody in a mass by Verdi, and the link between popular songs and religious themes is frequently closer than we might imagine. Years ago a naval chaplain was giving an illustrated talk to his ship's company, outlining the basic tenets of the Christian faith. One of the ratings operated the lantern slide projector and another a gramophone, on which he had to play suitable music to accompany each slide. On the New Testament he felt reasonably confident with carols and Easter hymns to twin with the story of Christ. It was some of the Old Testament material that had him stuck

and when the slide showing Adam and Eve appeared
on the screen, all he had been able to come up with was
'If You Were the Only Girl in the World'.

Where that might have been an acceptable burst of
inspiration, the same couldn't be said of the bellringer
in a Suffolk church who tried to liven up the services by
impromptu bursts on the church bells. One morning
matins was heralded by 'Three Blind Mice' and in spite
of being reprimanded after that, he responded to a
dismal collection in aid of the bell fund a few weeks
later by letting rip with, 'Put Another Nickel In', a
virtuoso performance that cost him his job.

Hymn titles, like Bibical texts, have a curious knack
of often conveying more than they intend to. In the last
century the organist at Marlborough College was adept
at selecting hymns that fell perfectly in line with the
mood of the school. One summer term Gloucestershire
played a cricket match against the school first eleven,
in which W.G. Grace was bowled first ball by one of the
boys. That evening the hymns in the chapel included
one with the line, 'The scanty triumphs grace hath won.'
After another match, this time against a visiting team
from Cheltenham College whose innings was ruined
for them by the work of two Marlborough bowlers
called Wood and Stone, the event was celebrated by the
singing of:

> The heathen in his blindness
> Bows down to wood and stone.

Less felicitous, and probably avoided by all astute school
chaplains and organists, is hymn 304 in the *Public
School Hymn Book*, by H. Bonar, which opens with the
lines:

> Go, labour on; spend, and be spent,
> Thy joy to do the Master's will;

and ends with a rousing final verse:

> Toil on, and in thy toil rejoice;
> For toil comes rest, for exile home;

Soon shalt thou hear the Bridegroom's voice,
The midnight cry, 'Behold, I come!'

A real boner for Bonar!

The rural dean of Bletchley, visiting the church at
Leighton Buzzard thirty years ago, lent a special
meaning to one of the hymns sung during the service
that contained a reference to 'the consuming fires of sin',
when the back of his surplice came into too close a
proximity with a candle and he was made all too aware
of Henry Newbold's 'sacred flame'.

An example of how disastrous the selection of the
wrong hymn can be comes from the tribulation of a
young soldier who, as best man at a friend's wedding,
took a particular liking to one of the hymns, 'O God of
Love, to Thee We Bow', and made a note of its number,
774 in the Methodist hymn book, so that it could be sung
at his own wedding a few weeks later. On the great day
he was a trifle late arriving at the church and barely
slipped into his pew before the organ announced the
arrival of his bride. With no time to check details, the
vicar did make the point, however, of whispering
hurriedly, 'Are you sure it's 774 you want?' Assured, he
began the service and the congregation sang with some
bewilderment:

Come, O Thou Traveller unknown,
Whom still I hold, but cannot see,
My company before is gone,
And I am left alone with Thee.
With Thee all night I mean to stay,
And wrestle till the break of day.

This was reckoned to be Wesley's favourite hymn, and
it's numbered 774 in the *Ancient and Modern Standard*
hymn book.

At a service held in a maternity hospital the chaplain
had invited the mothers-to-be to chose hymns they
would enjoy. One opted for 'What a Friend We Have in

111

Jesus', forgetting perhaps the peculiar significance of two of its lines:

> Are we weak and heavy-laden,
> Cumbered with a load of care?

A perpetual late-comer was greeted at matins one morning by the rest of the congregation singing, 'With Early Feet I Love to Appear among Thy Saints'.

And a sermon against the evils of alcohol, which ended with the exhortation that all beers, wines and spirits should be thrown into the river, was followed immediately by the hymn 'Shall We Gather at the River'.

It isn't every hymn writer who has been blessed with the gift of writing lucid verses and the inanities of some hymns were parodied by Dr T.R. Glover's lines:

> We know Thee not nor guess Thee,
> O vague beyond our dreams,
> We praise Thee not nor bless Thee,
> Dim source of all that seems.
> Unconscious be our witness,
> The music of the heart,
> O it becomes all itness
> If aught indeed Thou art!

Notable among the writers of religious music was John Mason Neale, who composed and translated the words of some of the most popular hymns and carols in the hymn book, among them 'Good King Wenceslas', 'Jerusalem the Golden' and 'O Happy Band of Pilgrims'. Neale had a genius for verse, and the story is told of a visit he made to John Keble at his Hampshire living of Hursley. Neale arrived early and was asked to wait while Keble finished some business, and passed the time translating one of Keble's poems in *The Christian Year* into Latin. When Keble came to meet him, Neale asked innocently, 'I always thought that your poems were entirely original.' 'And so they are,' said Keble, a bit put out. 'Well, what about this?' asked Neale, handing over his Latin version with a smile.

The friendship between the organist at St Margaret's, Westminster, and the policeman who regularly patrolled the area at night, also enjoyed a degree of friendly banter as they habitually met and exchanged goodnights with each other. One evening the policeman was not at their usual rendezvous and as he hurried up the street his friend called out, 'I nearly missed you tonight.' 'One beat late,' apologized the policeman. 'Oh, I thought it might have been one bar's interval,' said the organist, on which note they moved on – as must we.

BEHOLD THE BRIDEGROOM DRAWETH NIGH

H.L. Mencken had a lot to say about marriage:

> Love is the star men look up to as they walk along, and marriage is the coal-hole they fall into.
>
> Marriage is a romance in which the hero dies in the first chapter.
>
> Bigamy is having one wife too many. Monogamy is the same.

So did Helen Rowland, putting the opposite point of view:

> A husband is what is left of the lover once the nerve has been removed.
>
> Before marriage a man will lie awake all night thinking about something you said, after marriage he will fall asleep before you have finished saying it.
>
> When a girl marries she exchanges the attentions of many men for the inattentions of one.

Here is George Bernard Shaw on the subject: 'What God hath joined together no man shall ever put asunder: God will take care of that.'

While Sydney Smith took a more sanguine approach and said of marriage, 'It resembles a pair of shears, so joined that they cannot be separated; often moving in opposite directions, yet always punishing any one who comes between them.'

Yet in spite of these forebodings the sacrament of marriage has always been popular, even under the least promising of circumstances. Captain Woodward, an old sea captain from the last century, described in his memoirs how marriages used to be arranged for clerics working overseas, taking a specific example from one of his voyages down to the Gulf of Mexico:

I had on board thirteen young women, sent out by the Moravian Mission as wives for the missionaries stationed along the route. None of these young women knew which man they were to marry. Thirteen missionaries had simply written home for wives, and the society sent out thirteen young women educated for the purpose, each one supposed to be as good as the other! We arrived at St Kitts at three a.m., and the two missionaries, who had sent for wives thence, came on. I had the thirteen young women mustered up in a line, and one missionary said, 'I will have this one,' the other also took his choice, and both went off ashore with their new partners. The remaining eleven went down to bed again; whether pleased or disappointed I cannot say. At Antigua the same afternoon three were wanted and three selected as before, but the Antigua men had a better chance, as they had their view of the young women by daylight. The same process went on at each island as we passed, leaving me only two, after Barbadoes, to go on to Demarara. If I had been in the market I would quite as soon have had one of the twain that were left, and the last as any of them.

The success of these attachments was not recorded.

It wasn't only missionaries who put their trust in God to find a partner in life. Many years ago a correspondent to a daily newspaper wrote:

Have single women ever thought of praying for a husband? At 36 I went into a church and prayed.

'Look here, Lord,' I said, 'if you want me to be married it's up to you to find me a husband.'

Imagine my surprise three days later when a complete stranger (from that church) asked me to marry him.

And in days gone by hopeful maids used to offer up this prayer to St Catherine:

117

St Catherine, St Catherine – lend me thine aid, and
grant that I may never die an old maid.

A husband, St Catherine,
A good one, St Catherine;
But arn-a-one better than
Narn-a-one, St Catherine.

Sweet St Catherine,
A husband, St Catherine,
Handsome, St Catherine,
Rich, St Catherine,
Soon, St Catherine.

From Chic's 'Ladies in the Pulpit'

The story of one Lady Duncan was different in that she had found her mate, but looked for a way of sharing the news with him. The fortunate fellow was her physician, who had cared for her devotedly during a serious illness. While he was visiting her during her convalescence, she told him that she had made up her mind to get married, and when asked who he was, told the doctor he'd find the answer in II Samuel, 12.7. Opening his Bible at that verse he read what Nathan had said to David, 'Thou art the man.'

'Do you get the feeling that you're being mentally unfrocked?'

119

'That's not one, Simon – he's my
new mod curate!'

The Church itself lays down certain rules on whom
you may or may not marry, in the 'Table of Kindred and
Affinity', which is often displayed on a board in
churches. Below the statement on such a board in an
Essex church, which read, 'A man may not marry: his
wife's mother', someone had written, 'Lord have mercy
upon us and incline our hearts to keep this law.'

However, in an increasingly secular age, church
weddings today can lack some of the mystery and
divine significance of more devout times, which must
have made it particularly heartening for any clergymen thumbing through a past copy of *Woman* who
came across this letter:

My family are very pleased about my engagement
to a wonderful boy, but he has just confessed

'*The old vicar never criticized my flower arrangements!*'

something no one else knows. He doesn't believe in God. I worry about what my parents would think if they knew, but even more I worry about whether this would ruin our marriage. Have you heard of similar partnerships which have been successful?

Maybe it was a nagging anxiety like this which led to the reply given by a younger girl in answer to a question at her confirmation class. The bishop was visiting the parish and stayed to sit in on the final class before the service itself. Among his questions the vicar asked this little girl to define the state of matrimony. 'It's a time of awful torment which some of us must undergo before we are allowed to enter a better world,' she replied. 'No, no, my dear,' the vicar corrected, 'that isn't a definition of matrimony, but of Purgatory.' 'Let the child be,' interrupted the bishop. 'Perhaps she has been allowed to see the light.'

'I now pronounce you wife and man!'

The clergy themselves aren't above making elementary mistakes, even with something as commonplace as the marriage procedures. Instead of announcing in his notices one morning, 'I publish the banns,' a parish priest heard himself saying, 'I banish the pubs.' An absent-minded colleague who'd lost the banns-book yet again, had a stab at the announcements from memory and began, 'I publish the banns of marriage between ... between ...' 'Between the cushion and the seat, sir,' the organist hissed across at him for all to hear. And a nervous curate who remembered the names of those getting married, but not the order in which they were to go to the altar, announced of the first couple 'this is for the first time of asking', and of the second, 'this is for the third time of asking'. Then, realizing his mistake, he tried to remedy the matter by adding hastily, 'And the first shall be last, and the last shall be first.'

Verbal gaffes in the marriage service itself have led to some original acts of union in the presence of the Lord. The marriage of a bride whose groom had only been persuaded to have a church service after considerable arm-twisting, began by the vicar announcing, 'Dearly beloved, we are gathered together here in the sight of God, and in the fear of this congregation...'

Over the page in the Prayer Book lay another hurdle which proved the undoing of the priest who 'charged' the couple he was marrying, '...if either of you know any impediment, why ye may not be jawfully loined together in Matrimony, ye do now confess it.'

Matters aren't helped if one of the parties in the service has his or her book open on the wrong page. This happened to an unfortunate groom who found that he was having difficulty keeping track of what was happening, but put it down to beginner's nerves until it came to his responses. 'Wilt thou have this Woman to thy wedded wife... so long as ye both shall live?' asked the priest, a little tetchily, since he'd noticed that the groom's mind wasn't entirely on the matter in hand. 'I will renounce the Lord,' answered the groom in some bewilderment. 'If you insist on carrying on like this, I will have you turned out,' said the priest sharply. 'That is my desire,' replied the groom, now totally at a loss.

During a sermon preached at a marriage the elderly rector innocently told his congregation, 'Sometimes in a marriage, the couple have been known to get on top of each other...'

And it was a vicar's wife who telegrammed to a friend

on her wedding morning, 'Read I John 4.18'. Unfortunately the 'I' before 'John' was left out of the message at the other end, leaving the bride to seek the reference in St John's gospel. So instead of being comforted by the thought, in the epistle, 'There is no fear in love; but perfect love casteth out fear: because fear hath torment. He that feareth is not made perfect in love', she read with alarm, 'For thou hast had five husbands; and he whom thou now hast is not thy husband: in that saidst thou truly.'

From Australia comes the story of a wedding party that reached the church considerably the worse for wear. The bride, already heavily pregnant, chewed gum all the way up the nave and the groom had to be supported by two friends who were nearly as drunk as he was. With great reluctance, and only because of the lady's advanced condition, the priest agreed to proceed with the service, though not without registering his strong disapproval in his opening words, 'Dearly beloved, we are gathered together here in spite of God...'

During the last war an English vicar took great exception to a government form which included the term 'unmarried wife'. Airing his complaint publicly, he said, 'It seems to me to be a hint from the government that you should have an unmarried wife. It is a nasty hit at the sanctity of marriage. When I saw the phrase, I wondered what we were fighting for.'

Taking a stand against the easy-going attitude of the 1960s, one Warwickshire vicar attempted to restore some dignity by telling prospective married couples that he would refuse to marry them if they were more than five minutes late arriving for the service. 'It is not only inconvenient for me,' he explained. 'It is also a grave discourtesy to God.'

Back in the eighteenth century Jonathan Swift came to the timely rescue of a young couple who, through no fault of theirs, were in danger of being considerably later than this for their wedding. Swift had been out walking when a violent thunderstorm forced him to shelter under a tree. There he found the wedding party also taking refuge, the bride in tears at the thought of missing the service. 'Never mind, I'll marry you,' suggested the dean, to which they happily agreed. So while the heavens roared overhead, he took out his prayer book and performed the ceremony there and then. To complete formally the proceedings he also tore a page from his pocket book and composed a 'marriage certificate' which read:

Under a tree in stormy weather,
I married this man and woman together;
Let none but Him who rules the thunder
Sever this man and woman asunder.

A generation before Swift, Dr Robert South was once called from his bed on a bitter winter morning to marry a couple who had arrived unannounced and were waiting to see him. After hurrying to the church through the frosty air he found a couple well into their seventies and asked them crossly where the bride and groom were, and what they themselves were doing in the church. The old man answered that it was he and his elderly companion who wanted to be married. 'Married!' exclaimed South. 'Yes, married,' answered the old man. 'Better marry than do worse.' 'Go, get you gone, you silly old fools!' the doctor told them. 'Get home and do your worst,' and so hastened back to the warmth of his fire, berating the clerk who had called him for dragging him from his bed on such an errand.

In a more reflective mood, Bishop Stubbs, whose Oxford diocese encompassed the parish where South had this encounter, composed a riddle on marriage that contains its own period charm and which makes a fitting coda to these thoughts on the subject:

Why is a man making a morning call like one taking the first four steps, or sometimes the fifth step, to matrimony?

1. He comes to a door (adore)
2. He seeks a bell (belle)
3. And produces a ring
4. And gives his name to the maid
5. And sometimes gets let in

WITHIN THE CHURCH'S SACRED FOLD

Aformer bishop of Southwark summed up many contemporary attitudes to church-going when he referred to what he regarded as the 'four-wheeler' religion practised by a large number of the laity in his diocese. The first 'four-wheeler' he said was the pram in which a child is brought to baptism. The second is the taxi in which he or she comes to the church to be married. And the third is the hearse in which they come to be buried. Couple this with the story of the man who explained his reasons for not going to church and you'll discover the other side of the coin. 'The first time I went to church, they threw water in my face,' he complained. 'The second time they tied me to a woman I've had to keep ever since.' 'That's right,' said the parson to whom he was speaking, 'and the next time you go to church they'll throw dirt at you.' Add Christmas, possibly Easter and maybe a confirmation, and there you'll have the pillars on which much of today's church-going is based.

However, even those who don't go to church have developed means of conveying their respect to the Lord. Dr Johnson said of an acquaintance, who was a case in point, 'Campbell is a good man, a pious man. I am afraid he has not been inside a church for many years, but he never passes a church without pulling off his hat. This shows that he has good principles.'

Aubrey Menen pointed to other reasons for paying attention to the Almighty: 'So she goes to church. It's cheaper than the psychologist and more convenient, being only once a week.'

One of the earlier bishops of Hereford, dining with a peer of the realm who lived in the diocese, was told by his host, 'I don't know if you've noticed, Bishop, but I never go to church.' The bishop replied that he had noticed. The peer, by now well into a decanter of port, continued, 'And I'll tell you why I don't go – the place is full of hypocrites!' 'My dear sir,' said the bishop smiling, 'please don't let that put you off. I'm sure we can make room for one more.'

His lordship's excuse is matched by another evergreen one - other commitments. Two fishermen, piecing together their tackle on a river bank one Sunday morning heard the sound of the church bells calling to them across the meadow. 'We really ought to be in matins,' acknowledged one. 'Well, I wouldn't be able to go, anyway,' said his friend, casting his line, 'my wife's ill.'

Another anxious Anglican asked his vicar whether it was a sin to own two cars and a boat and received a reply that forestalled further questioning: 'That all depends on where they're parked on a Sunday morning.'

Clearly the concept of regular Sunday church-going has drifted so far from the lives of some people that they have difficulty in still coming to terms with it. A party of tourists who were visiting Winchester during the summer were delayed in heavy Saturday traffic while travelling to the city and reached the cathedral, the last stop in their itinerary, just as it was closing. Hearing that they were staying overnight, the verger reminded them helpfully that it would reopen early the following morning, to which one was overheard remarking, 'Well, what do you know! This place is even open on a Sunday.'

And from Canterbury comes a companion comment from a visitor walking into the cathedral during a choir rehearsal who asked, 'Say, do they still hold services here?'

Someone more attuned to the workings of the Church and the value of its buildings both spiritually and structurally was one Mr Ivor Bulmer-Thomas who, as chairman of the Executive Committee of the Historic Churches Preservation Trust, once explained his own criterion for distinguishing between individual churches, which seemed eminently English: 'When I visit a fine old church I ask myself, "Has this given me as much pleasure as a glass of sherry?" If the answer is yes, as it nearly always is, I slip half a crown into the box.' Now what could be fairer that that?

Unfortunately not all church visitors display the same qualities of discernment, nor indeed set such high store by what they find inside. The vicar of a Suffolk church felt obliged to draw up and post a set of rules of good conduct in his ancient church after finding a party of brass rubbers frying up their lunch on a camping stove at the altar rails.

Furthermore, some visitors' sense of dress has far out-stripped (literally) that of the majority of cathedral deans and chapters. An elderly canon at Durham Cathedral had rigidly fixed views on what was fitting attire to be worn inside his particular House of God, though ones that showed little understanding of the modern lady's wardrobe. Told by one of the cathedral guides that a woman had just walked inside dressed in a bikini, his reply was forthright and unbending: 'Then tell her to take it off!'

Twenty-odd years ago an irate correspondent to *The Sunday Times* informed the editor, 'I saw two girls smoking cigarettes and one man smoking a pipe in Coventry Cathedral. At Whitsun last year I saw two teenagers embracing in St George's Chapel, Windsor. Three teenage girls were playing a portable radio in Lincoln Cathedral. I remembered Noël Coward's line in *Cavalcade*, "Something is happening to England and I, for one, don't like it."'

Some few years ago I had been doing a number of recordings for the Scripture Union in connection with Ladybird Books, reading Bible stories for children. It so happened that the television series in which I took part immediately after the recordings was called *Third Time Lucky* and for once I was not playing a parson. On almost my first appearance in the series, I had to put my feet in some freezing cold water and then

'Whichever daily is in greatest need.'

smartly withdraw them exclaiming, 'This water's absolutely bloody freezing!' The broadcast elicited a deluge of mail, telling me how ghastly it had been that I had said 'By Our Lady', which really hadn't occurred to me, because one doesn't think of 'bloody' being a blasphemy any more than 'blinking' ('by Our Lady's

131

skin'), or 'Blimy'/'Gor blimy!' ('God blind me'). After all most of us say 'goodbye' without realizing that it's really 'God be with you'. Be that as it may, such was the protest over what I'd said, that the Scripture Union asked me to withdraw my name from the recordings, which left me feeling somewhat miffed.

A week later I picked up Tommy Thomas, who was at that time Dean of Melbourne Cathedral, and drove him up the motorway to meet the Dean of Lincoln. En route, he looked out of the window as we made our way up the A1, and said, 'Oh, look over there, Derek, there's a bloody marvellous view.'

'Dean,' I said, 'for saying that I've been struck off the Scripture Union. You ought to be excommunicated.'

Back in church, even those who do find themselves seated in a pew and taking part in a service aren't always aware of the correct way to conduct themselves. The wife of a vicar, seated behind a visitor to their church one Sunday morning, became exasperated at the woman's habit of rustling through the hymn book page by page while her husband was delivering his sermon. Unable to endure the distraction any longer, she tapped her shoulder and whispered tartly, 'Excuse me. This is St Peter's - not St Vitus.'

Two other visitors to a different church came one Sunday to join in the christening which was forming part of that morning's worship. They arrived just after the service had started and stood in the doorway in some bewilderment until a churchwarden proffered hymn and prayer books and asked, 'Are you with the christening party?' 'No,' said the husband apprehensively, 'I'm with the Woolwich.'

Regular attendance can be boosted too with a little imagination, as was proved at Holy Communion in Chelmsford Cathedral once. Double the number of communicants attended the service following the announcement that breakfast would be provided at a nominal charge after the service. You can also put off fewer people by a little judicious planning ahead. The flower guild responsible for decorating a West Country church for its Harvest Festival foresaw problems with a donation of locally caught fish that would have to lie in place for several days, and took the wise step of soaking them in eau de cologne before adding them to the display.

Subtler methods of drawing the wavering into church have been employed, as well, though to questionable effect. A London vicar suggested to the people of his parish that those who took communion in his church were less likely to catch disease from the service than those who attended free church services. He reasoned that the communion wine served by the Church of England was more like to inhibit the spread of germs than the non-alcoholic wine used by the free churches. One wonders what weight an argument like that would carry in the current atmosphere of alarm about AIDS?

People can be put off going to church in winter because of the cold, though here too the resourcefulness of some members of the clergy can be a potent antidote. When the heating system failed in a Northamptonshire church, the vicar kept the congregation's blood moving by marching them round the church twice while singing, 'Forward! Be Our Watchword,/Steps and voices join'd'. Although this display of muscular Christianity achieved its aim, the result was over-shadowed by the failure of the sidesman to ring the bell to announce the end of the second lap, with the consequence that at least one elderly spinster arrived back in her pew exhausted and barely in time for the Gloria, after circumnavigating the churchyard a record fifteen times.

Perhaps one of the most delightful calls to pray came from the officer on duty at a naval shore base who had the responsibility of arranging that Sunday's church parade. To the men lined up in front of him he bellowed the command, 'Roam out the fallen Catholics.'

And it may well have been intimations of similar transgressions that led an elderly and otherwise unquestionably devout member of a church congregation to bow her head whenever the devil's name was mentioned. When asked why she did this, she replied with perfect candour, 'You never know. It might come in handy.'

One of the principal reasons for going to church is to pray of course, and here the Anglican can put himself on a firm footing with the Lord; and in some cases, almost as importantly, display his piety to his fellow worshippers. One past-master at this latter technique was asked by a friend how it was that he invariably managed to look up from his private exchange with the Almighty, which was always conducted into the upturned hat that he respectfully held on his knees, at just the right moment. Revealing his secret, he explained, 'When I've read "Lock & Co, Hatters, St James's Street, London" to myself three times over, I know it's time to look up.'

Public displays like this don't meet with universal approval – at least they don't outside a church. The well-known Roman Catholic writer, Father Martindale, was reading his breviary on top of a bus one day when he was noticed by a fellow passenger seated beside him, who told her companion in loud, disapproving tones, 'When I pray I go into an upper room and shut the door.' Turning round to address her, Father Martindale replied, 'And then you come into a bus and tell the world about it.' It makes you wonder what her response would have been if she'd overheard a comment that appeared in print in a letter in a Sunday newspaper which read, 'I am not a nudist but I always say my prayers in the nude. It seems to bring me nearer to God.'

There seems little doubt, though, that that lady and, I dare say, a good many like her would have taken issue with another newspaper correspondent who suggested that the BBC should stop allowing women to read prayers and conduct services for transmission. 'Women in this capacity lack the humble approach,' he continued. 'They don't *pray* to Almighty God, they *demand* him in the irritating "talking down to" manner of a schoolmistress.' As far as this listener was concerned, this reduced the services 'to the level of mere recitation'.

Over the centuries God has been *demanded* of by Christians, fully convinced that prayer is a convenient hot-line to getting what you want. How many fishermen have cast a hopeful line while sending up thoughts similar to the angler's prayer:

> I pray you, Lord, send me a fish
> So big that even I,
> When speaking of it afterwards,
> Shall have no cause to lie.

Or how many weary workers have staggered into bed with thoughts like these:

> Lord, send us weeks of Sundays
> A saint's day every day
> Shirts gratis and for nothing
> No work and double pay.

A priest flying during rough weather was sitting alongside a woman who finally lost her nerve after a particularly violent patch of turbulence and grabbed his arm asking, 'Can't you do something?' 'Madam,' he replied disdainfully, 'I'm in sales, not management.'

A fellow cleric under similar conditions was asked by a nervous hostess, 'Please do something... you know, something religious!' Unstrapping himself from his seat, the priest obliged and walked down the plane taking a collection.

The presence of bishops doesn't necessarily bring greater security either, as the crew of a Jumbo flying the Atlantic discovered when one of their engines failed an hour and a half short of Heathrow. One of the bishops, aware that something was up, told the senior steward comfortingly that he and three colleagues were on board. The message was conveyed to the flight deck, from where the steward returned with the reply, 'The pilot is much obliged, Bishop. But he says he'd still rather have that fourth engine.'

Self-interest in prayers can seldom have been more blatantly expressed than by one of George I's MPs, John Ward, who addressed these words to the Divine ears:

> O Lord, Thou knowest that I have nine houses in the City of London, and that I have lately purchased an estate in fee simple in Essex. I beseech Thee to preserve the two counties of Middlesex and Essex from fires and earthquakes. And, as I have also a mortgage in Hertfordshire, I beg Thee also to have an eye of compassion on that county, and for the rest of the counties Thou mayest deal with them as Thou are pleased. O Lord, enable the Banks to answer all their bills, and make all debtors good men. Give prosperous voyage and safe return to the Mermaid sloop because I have not insured it. And because Thou hast said, 'The days of the wicked are but short,' I trust that Thou wilt not forget Thy promise, as I have an estate in reversion on the death of the profligate young man, Sir J.L. . . . Keep my friends from sinking, preserve me from thieves and housebreakers, and make all my servants so honest and faithful that they may always attend to my interests, and never cheat me out of my property night or day.

One of his successors in the Mother of Parliaments was observed deep in prayer by a younger colleague whenever the Commons gathered for its regular devotional offices. Asked once whether he prayed for the House, the older man replied, 'No. I take a look at the House and pray for the country.'

One group of worshippers who would have shared his opinion about their MP were Conservative voters in North Devon, who had found their candidate pipped at the post by a Liberal politician named Jeremy Thorpe, who'd won the seat with a majority of under four hundred. When the vicar of one parish in the constituency offered prayers for the recently elected MP, there was a sizeable proportion of the congregation who registered their displeasure.

Praying after the election wasn't likely to have had much impact, of course, but the timely intervention of the Almighty has been sought on countless occasions. Here are just two. During a great drought in the mid-seventeenth century, a Puritan preacher offered up these words:

> Lord, there have been come semblances and overtures, Lord, of rain. The clouds indeed were gathered together but they were suddenly dispersed. Lord, Lord Thou knowest that the kennels of the street yield an unsavoury smell!

A vicar travelling on a Newcastle to London express discovered after he had boarded it that the train didn't stop at York, where he wanted to get out. So, calling on all his powers of persuasion, he began praying for the train to slow down. Fellow passengers were amused at this until their lack of faith turned to wonder as it did indeed start to brake as they approached the city. Apologizing to his fellow travellers for any inconvenience he might have caused, the vicar opened the carriage door when the train was almost stationary and jumped out. Asked to explain himself later, he said, 'I was booked to address the British Sailors' Society in York and didn't want to be late. I am a firm believer in the power of prayer.'

Another staunch advocate of prayer was apparently

the Duke of Cambridge, at one time commander-in-chief of the British army. It is related that in the middle of family prayers at Chatsworth, where he was once staying, he announced very loudly to the assembled household, while they were all on their knees, 'A damned good custom this.' No doubt many shared his opinion, although in some households the practice and the preaching still remained on rather distant terms with each other.

An unfortunate guest in a large country house was late down on his first morning and found that the prayers led by the master of the house had already started. He tried to be as inconspicuous as he could and took the nearest vacant chair. 'O Lord, before whom all are equal...' intoned the head of the household before pausing as he was about to read from the Scriptures, to beckon the late arrival to him. When he was close enough, he whispered, 'You are sitting among the servants.'

As J.M. Barrie said in *The Admirable Crichton*, 'His Lordship may compel us to be equal upstairs, but there will never be equality in the servants' hall.'

BLESSED
ARE THE
PURE
IN HEART

Many years ago somebody said that Wesley-ans had all the fire and the Baptists all the water, while Church people had all the starch. That starch may have become less rigid today, but traces of it can still be found dotted through parishes all over the country.

Not that many years ago discipline and piety went hand in hand. A correspondent to the *Edinburgh Evening News* probably expressed a widely held opinion on corporal punishment, when he wrote, 'I would put first on the list the sloppy sentimental politicians who have outlawed the use of the "cat". At the time of Culloden 500 strokes of the cat were quite common in the Duke of Cumberland's army for such offences as looting. We pay a heavy price for departing from Christian standards.'

A fellow sympathizer found fault even with an example set in the Bible. Mounting the lectern to read a Christmas lesson from the second chapter of St Luke, a landowner with extensive farming interests prefaced the apostle's description of the shepherds leaving their flocks to see the newly-born child in the stable with the remark, 'I would just like to say before reading this lesson that if they'd been my shepherds I'd have sacked them.'

Another correspondent, writing on the same theme, took issue with the humility advocated by the Church in relation to the peoples of the empire. 'I observe that in the form of prayer for use on January 3 we are to ask forgiveness "because we have indulged in national arrogance, finding satisfaction in our power over others rather than in our ability to serve them"', read the letter to *The Times*. 'May I point out', continued the writer, 'that this is a severe censure on all public servants in India, the Crown Colonies, and the Mandated Territories? What grounds are there for stating that this large body of public servants have grossly failed in their duty?'

In those bygone days few Anglicans had any doubt on which side of the fence the Lord stood, as Clarence Day wrote in *Life With Father*, 'Aside from a few odd words in Hebrew, I took it completely for granted that God had never spoken anything but the most dignified English.' These sentiments would have been shared, I suspect, by the correspondent to the *Daily Mirror* who wrote, 'I trust that England knows more of her Bible than to believe a Messiah can come from America.'

At home too there were some stern words that added a fresh gloss to the Protestant work ethic when they appeared in the *Daily Record*: 'It makes me highly indignant to see so many heathen, agnostics, sceptics and atheists taking advantage of a Christian holiday.' The correspondent went on to suggest that people should be stopped from having a few days off at Easter until we remembered as a nation that 'this is a Christian festival'.

The sanctity of Sunday itself seemed under threat forty years ago, long before the present idea of Sunday trading was ever mooted. A Sussex parishioner wrote to his local newspaper, 'There will be no future peace unless righteousness is firmly established. As a start, why should not the whole Church make an appeal to the railway companies and the public to stop Sunday excursions?'

There were worthy intentions in the mind of a young man, recently arrived in London for the first time, who asked his new vicar in confidence whether he thought he could live an honest Christian life on twenty-five pounds a week. 'My dear boy, that's all you'll be able to do,' replied the vicar.

Maintaining standards that were fitting in the eyes of the Lord and His Church posed other fundamental problems. Were whale steaks proper Friday fare, enquired one anxious Anglican of his bishop? A lady who worked during the week was troubled at the prospect of hanging her washing on a line on Sunday.

And a keen wordsmith, worried perhaps by memories of what had happened in Eden over the Tree of Knowledge, asked the editor of the *Christian Herald*, 'Would you kindly give your opinion whether doing crossword competitions is displeasing to God?' To which the editor responded, 'I can well believe that such competitions are entertaining and instructive, and certainly there is not the slightest reason from the Christian point of view that you should not indulge in what is, surely, a perfectly innocent pastime when no money transactions are involved.'

Words from the Bible quoted in an unsuitable context led to an edict from the BBC Head of Light Entertainment fifty years ago, which banned the misuse of the Scriptures. The problem arose after one radio comedian said of a joke that hadn't been well received by the studio audience, 'That fell on stony ground.' Following that a list of quotations was drawn up with clear instructions that only preachers and commentators were to use them on the air. Among those turns of phrase lost to the listening public were, 'A voice crying in the wilderness', 'An eye for an eye', 'The salt of the earth', 'Man shall not live by bread alone', 'Sufficient unto the day is the evil thereof', 'Where your treasure is there will your heart be also'.

Twenty-five years later, when I was first contracted by the BBC Television Light Entertainment Department, similar rules applied. In particular there were five subjects which we were not allowed on any account to mention in comedy programmes. They were: religion, the Royal Family, physical disability, racial prejudice, and indeed sexual variations. A few years later, Frank Muir, who until then had been Head of Television Situation Comedy, left the BBC to join commercial television where no such strictures applied. He said the first line he was going to write when he got there was, '"For Christ sakes," said the Queen, "that one-legged nigger's a poof"'!

Hand in hand with decorous language goes decorous behaviour, both inside and outside church. A West Country clergyman, staying alone in a hotel, was invited to share a table in the dining room with a single lady to whom he had been introduced before the meal. They enjoyed a convivial dinner at the end of which the waitress offered them a pot of coffee, which they accepted. As she was making a note on her bill, though, she paused with the germ of thought which materialized in the statement, 'No. You've got separate rooms. You shouldn't really share a pot. I'd better bring two.'

There are some congregations that can be only too quick to wave a finger of reproof when their parsons step out of line in matters of no greater seriousness than this. In the days when the horse was still the only form of road transport, Samuel Wilberforce received a complaint that one of his rectors drove his carriage in tandem, to the scandal of the pious and the discredit of the Church. The bishop tackled the rector about this and he replied, 'But your Lordship drives two horses, and the only difference between us is that your Lordship drives them side by side and I drive them one in front of the other.' This obliged Wilberforce to illustrate his answer, and putting his hands together as if in prayer, he said, 'When I place my hands thus you will perceive that I place them in an attitude becoming a Christian and a bishop, but when I place them thus' (extending the fingers of both hands one in front of the other and putting his thumb to his nose) 'you will admit that the case is quite different.'

Complaints to Wilberforce from a deputation of parishioners enraged by what they considered to be Romish practices in their church were met with the same suave response. The leader of the group told Wilberforce that if he had his way, he would have the priests responsible hanged. 'That I can scarcely do,' replied the bishop. 'The only power I have is to suspend them.'

The influence of the Church of Rome caused concern to a churchwarden at Felstead who expressed his doubts about his vicar to Bishop Blomfield, as he was disrobing after a confirmation service. 'What specific allegation do you wish to make?' asked Blomfield. 'Well, my Lord, he kisses his stole,' the warden replied in disgust. Blomfield was less concerned and only suggested, 'Well, that is better than if he stole his kisses.'

If this infiltration wasn't bad enough for these dyed-in-the-wool traditionalists, the prospect of women preaching to them was quite beyond the Pale. Dr Johnson didn't think much of the idea and said, 'a woman's preaching is like a dog's walking on his hinder legs. It is not done well; but you are surprised to find it done at all.' And from the early part of this century come these lines of defiance, tinged with resignation:

> Let them adorn our parlour and our kitchen.
> Let them infest the study and the stage.
> Be doctors, dentists, occupy a niche in
> The manliest professions of the age.
> Women as jurors? Well, we'll try to gulp it
> Down with the rest because the age is brisk.
> But we won't have a woman in our pulpit.
> That is too great a risk!

Anglican laity have set ideas on what they want from their Church as well, and campaigns to ginger them up don't always attain the desired result, as this parishioner remarked to his parish priest after a recent stewardship campaign: 'I've been through a good many of these missions, Vicar,' he said, 'and they're all alike. While it's on, everything is "Glory be to the Father and to the Son and to the Holy Ghost." But once it's over, it's back to "As it was in the beginning is now and ever shall be, world without end. Amen."'

The introduction of revised services has run into

144

some pretty stubborn resistance in many conservative parishes and seems to have caused considerable confusion in others. This remark shared by a couple of businessmen sums up several widely-held opinions: 'The way the Church of England is going, we'll have to form a New Centre Church. They talk about unity and when they announce the Lord's Prayer you have to say "Which one?"'

Even the Almighty Himself can't escape blameless, judging by the censure of at least one member of his flock, who suggested that in view of the appalling harvest that year the regular Harvest Festival services should either be cancelled or changed in some way as a mark of disappointment.

A bishop visiting the garden of a country house that had been made over to the public after many years of neglect found God at fault there. Wandering round the immaculately-kept gardens he found an elderly gardener in one of the greenhouses to whom he remarked, 'What wonderful results can be achieved by God and a gardener working together.' The gardener agreed with him and added as an afterthought, 'But you should have seen what it was like when God had it all to himself.'

It's this ability to look God in the eye, man to Maker, that characterizes the relationship some of His contemporary children have with Him. The Church isn't slow either in adopting this matter-of-fact, no-nonsense approach. Forty years ago the *News Chronicle* announced, 'A new edition of the Bible, especially written for the man in the street and illustrated with pictures of tanks, marching armies and aeroplanes, is to be published soon.'

The Rev. James Russell, the Sporting Parson, who was vicar of Swimbridge, once advertised for a curate as follows, 'Wanted – a curate for Swimbridge, must be a gentleman of moderate and orthodox views.' Some of the parishioners were puzzled about the meaning of the term 'orthodox' so they consulted the Parish Clerk. 'Ah,' said the latter, 'I think it means a chap as can ride well to hounds'!

A vicar seen out shooting by one of his parishioners and later challenged by her with the comment, 'I never heard that the apostles went out shooting,' simply replied, 'That's quite correct. You see, they spent all their spare time fishing.'

Another member of the cloth took a hard-headed look at the state of the world today and, writing about this in his parish magazine, concluded that if Moses was to come down from Mt Sinai now, the two tablets he'd be bringing with him would be aspirins.

The efforts to blend the Church into modern life have necessarily resulted in some slight blurring at the edges, displayed in one Anglican's attempt to buy a copy of the *Church Times*. He called at the newsagent where he regularly bought his copy, asked for it and was told that it hadn't come in. By way of compensation the assistant pointed out, 'Some of the other comics are late getting here too.' A different customer, this term in search of a particular book of theology, asked in a bookshop where he should look for it. The assistant looked blank and could only offer the suggestion that he hunt round the shelves, adding, 'When it comes to theology, you've just got to trust to luck.'

One seeker after truth who thought he was on firmer ground than that must have had a bit of a shock when he applied for a Bible. A native of Ghana, he had noticed the words 'ask and it shall be given you' in a copy of the good book distributed in his country by the Folkestone Biblical Society, so he sent a letter to the Folkestone town council asking if they could let him have a copy too. Having no Bibles to hand, they sent him a letter of thanks accompanied by a copy of the town guide.

More reassuring to the God-fearing was the automatic expression of old Christian standards that

'Of course, I'm just a Monday painter.'

came from an assistant in a bookshop in Kent who, when asked for a book of conversion tables, answered apologetically, 'I'm afraid we haven't got any. The nearest we stock in that line is the Bible.'

Just as heartening must have been the news of a ninety-three-year-old grandmother who returned to these shores after emigrating to Argentina two years earlier, and explained that her change of heart was due largely to the fact that out there the radio didn't broadcast 'Lift Up Your Hearts' or any other religious services in English.

Even in adversity there are still some who refuse to let their adherence to time-honoured values slip. Members of the Northern Area of the Church of England Vergers' Guild, meeting for one of their annual conferences, heard complaints about their declining earnings but resisted the current of the times and never even considered taking strike action. As one of their spokesmen explained, 'It would have been beneath the dignity of our calling to do anything so vulgar.'

All the same the Church is aware of the challenge it faces, brought home in stark reality by announcements like that from a parish in Cumbria where a list of organizations affiliated to the church was being prepared and included the Young Wives until someone pointed out that the Young Wives had been disbanded since most of the members had gone to join the Over Sixties.

There is the challenge of faith itself, expressed by the limerick:

> There was a young man whose piety
> Compelled him to join a society.
> He vowed many things,
> And wore medals on strings,
> But he died in great doubt and anxiety.

And the story of the walker who fell over a cliff at night and through a freak of good fortune managed to break his descent by grabbing hold of a tree root near the top. There he hung in the dark shouting, 'Is anyone down there?' 'Yes,' answered a voice far below. 'I am down here. You can trust me. Let yourself go. I am God.' The walker clung there still, stunned it seemed by what he had heard. At last he shouted again, 'Is anybody else down there?'

Or the nagging awareness of sin, voiced by a lady who confessed to her vicar, 'I suppose I ought to admit to you that I spend a lot of my time looking into the mirror and saying to myself that I am getting prettier every day.' 'Let me comfort you,' said the vicar. 'That is not a sin at all, only a mistake.'

There is the constant worry about money as well, not

helped by the perennial reluctance of so many to contribute so little. A woman collecting donation envelopes
for Christian Aid called at one house to be told, 'I'm
sorry, I can't give you anything, our dog ate the
envelope you left.' 'That doesn't matter,' replied the
collector, 'I've got a spare envelope here.' 'That's no
good,' said the householder quickly, 'he'd only eat that
one too.'

A young man collecting on behalf of the Salvation
Army offered his tin to an elderly man sitting over a
pint of beer in a pub and said, 'I'm collecting for the
Lord.' To which the old man answered, 'Well, you'd
better give that to me then. I'll be seeing him before you,
lad!'

If Anglicanism can be said to reflect any single
feature of the English as seen by other nations, it must
be that quality of national tolerance, indifference or
impartiality, call it what you will. An Englishman
watching the annual Rangers–Celtic match in Scotland
threw himself into the game and cheered loudly whenever a goal was scored, no matter which team had
kicked the ball into the net. At half-time a Scotsman
who'd been keeping an eye on him since the kick-off,
leaned over and asked, 'Good God, man. Haven't you
any religion at all?' A question which can only be
capped by the man at Speaker's Corner who assured
his audience in terms worthy of many of the laity,
'Thank God I'm an atheist.'

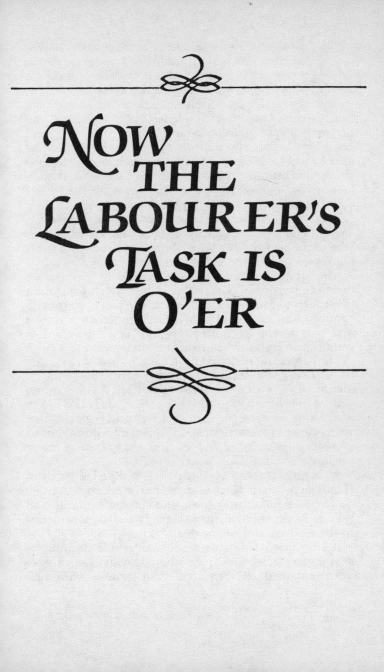

NOW THE LABOURER'S TASK IS O'ER

As far as Sydney Smith was concerned Heaven consists of 'eating *pâté de fois gras* to the sound of trumpets', and even in death Anglicans are not above enjoying a respectful chuckle.

A vicar of a Surrey parish who noticed a dead donkey lying in a field near his church, left behind after a group of gypsies had been camping there, rang the local council to report the matter. The official to whom he spoke answered waggishly that his understanding was that it was the duty of the vicar to bury the dead. 'That's as may be,' replied the vicar, 'but I thought the least I could do would be to inform the next of kin.'

Local authorities have been known to cause different sorts of confusion with respect to the dead themselves. One of the regional water authorities once sent a letter addressed to 'The Occupier, Cemetery, Church Road...' A fire at a crematorium led to a local newspaper headline that read 'Blaze closes crematorium'. And a mourner coming out of another local authority crematorium on a cold winter day slipped on some ice and was heard to mutter crossly, 'You'd think they would sprinkle a few ashes around here, wouldn't you?'

The culprit responsible for a Cambridgeshire vicar's tireless search among his parish records has yet to be identified. The vicar in question noticed a stone in the wall of his churchyard that bore the initials HWP. For months he combed through archives and registers in a vain attempt to identify the unknown parishioner until a sudden access of inspiration suggested a more prosaic meaning – hot water pipe.

A former Bishop of Bath and Wells, Dr Edward Henderson, when opening a crematorium commented, 'A great deal of money is expended upon funerals and that, in itself, seems to me to betray a lack of confidence in the resurrection of the dead.'

It's on tombstones that a considerable amount of that money goes, and from where the last laugh is so often obtained. A Bradford man, whose wife had

'Your five minutes is up, Mr Brearley.'

recently passed on, commissioned a headstone from a local monumental mason with the inscription, 'She was thine.' Some weeks later he heard that the stone was finished and had been put in place; so he went to see it and noticed immediately that the inscription was wrong, reading as it did, 'She was thin.' He rang the mason as soon as he was home and complained, 'You've left off the "e".' The mason was full of apologies and promised he would attend to the matter as soon as possible. True to his word he made the correction and called the customer to say that all was well. However, visiting the cemetery a second time he found that this wasn't strictly true, for the inscription now read, 'E, she was thin.'

Before browsing through a selection of epitaphs composed with the cemetery firmly in mind, let's have a look at some written, more tongue in cheek, by the deceased themselves, and seldom used. This was an activity in which American film stars featured prominently and theirs are some of the wittiest:

On the whole I'd rather be in Philadelphia.

W.C. Fields

Well, I've played everything but a harp.

Lionel Barrymore

Back to the silents.

Clark Gable

This is too deep for me.

Hedy Lamarr

This is just my lot.

Frederic March

Did you hear about my operation?

Warner Baxter

All my old junk gone to the storehouse,
Here I am, God, starting for your house.
In order to prevent possibility of ruction
Am bringing you back your original production.

George Arliss

The art of the epitaph writer is long and distinguished and many of the greatest names in English verse have applied their talents to it, if not always for the immortality of stone. Here's Byron on Viscount Castlereagh:

Posterity will ne'er survey
A nobler grave than this:
Here lie the bones of Castlereagh:
Stop, traveller, and piss.

And Lady Mary Wortley Montagu (and Alexander Pope) on two lovers from Stanton Harcourt in Oxfordshire, who were killed by lightning – first Lady M.W.:

Here lies John Hughes and Sarah Drew.
Perhaps you'll say, what's that to you?
Believe me, friend, much may be said
On this poor couple that are dead.
On Sunday next they should have married;
But see how oddly things have carry'd,
On Thursday last it rain'd and lighten'd,
These tender lovers sadly frighten'd
Shelter'd beneath the cocking hay
In hopes to pass the storm away.
But the bold thunder found them out
(Commission'd for that end no doubt)
And seizing on their trembling breath,
Consign'd them to the shades of death.
Who knows if 'twas was not kindly done?
For had they seen the next year's sun,
A beaten wife and cuckold swain
Had jointly curs'd the marriage chain.
Now they are happy in their doom,
For P. has wrote upon their tomb.

And what P. wrote was rather more succinct:

Here lie two lovers, who had the mishap
Tho' very chaste people, to die of a clap.

While John Gay composed for himself this couplet:

Life is a jest, and all things show it.
I thought so once; but now I know it.

The epitaph for the couple in the thunderstorm touches
on one of the most fruitful areas in which the epitaph
has flourished, those composed for victims of
accidents. Famous among these is the one that records
the sad shooting of an army officer:

Sacred to the memory of
Major James Brush
who was killed by accidental discharge of
a pistol by his orderly.
14th April 1831
Well done thou good and faithful servant

Another lightning victim was remembered in the lines:

Here lies a man who was killed by lightning
He died when his prospects seemed to be brightening.
He might have cut a flash in this world of trouble,
But the flash cut him, and he lies in the stubble.

The heavens held further perils, judging from this:

Here lies I -
Jonathan Fry -
Killed by a sky -
Rocket in my eye-
Socket.

And if there weren't things landing on you, you could
also do some unhappy landing of your own:

The Lord saw good, I was lopping off wood
And down fell from the tree.
I met with a check, and broke my neck
And so Death lopped off me.

Falling into the forerunner of the septic tank didn't
do you much good either:

Here lyeth ye body of Martin Hyde.
He fell down a midden and gievously dy'd.
James Hyde his brother fell down another,
They now lie interr'd side by side.

Water alone could finish you off as well:

Sudden and unexpected was the end,
Of our esteemed and beloved friend.
He gave all his friends a sudden shock,
By one day falling into Sunderland Dock.

Erected to the memory of
John MacFarlane
Drown'd in the Water of Leith
By a few affectionate friends.

Sacred to the memory of Hester Fisher of
Waterhouse, also of Anne Rothery wife of
N.P. Rothery, R.N. and of Elizabeth Ann Rothery

their daughter, who were unfortunately drowned at Chepstow on the evening of Saturday Septr. 20th 1812, after hearing a sermon from Philippians 1st chapter 21st verse.

Even seeking medical aid could kill you off in some instances:

> Here lies the body of Mary Ann Lowder
> She burst while drinking a seidlitz powder.
> Called from this world to her heavenly rest,
> She could have waited till it effervesced.

> Here lie I with my three daughters
> Who died drinking Cheltenham waters.
> If we had stuck to Epsom Salt,
> We should not sleep in this cold vault.

> Here lies the body of
> Samuel Young
> who came here and died
> for the benefit of his health

Another rich source of inspiration are those epitaphs written for followers of a particular trade. Here's one for a watchmaker:

> Here lies in a horizontal position the outside case of
> Thomas Hinde
> clock and watch maker.
> Who departed this life wound up
> in hope of being taken in hand
> by his Maker and being
> thoroughly cleaned repaired and
> set a-going in the world to come.
> On the 15th of August 1836
> in the nineteenth year of his life.

Now a pastry cook:

> Beneath this dust lies the mouldering crust
> Of Eleanor Batchelor Shoven.
> Well versed in the arts of pies, puddings, and tarts
> And the lucrative trade of the oven.

When she lived long enough she made her last puff,
A puff by her husband much praised.
And now she does lie and makes a dirt pie
And hopes that her crust will be raised.

And finally a domestic servant:

Here lies
John James Cook
of Newby
Who was a faithful
servant
to his master
and an
upright downright
honest man
1760

While not a trade, the epitaph for a keen cricketer
records what probably occupied his keenest attention:

I bowl'd, I struck, I caught, I stopp'd
Sure life's a game of cricket;
I block'd with care, with caution popp'd
Yet death has hit my wicket.

A lot of epitaph writers have had fun working round
some of their subjects' names, as these examples show:

Here in this grave there lies a Cave,
We call a Cave a Grave, –
If Cave be Grave and Grave be Cave,
Then reader judge, I Crave,
Whether doth Cave here lie in Grave,
Or Grave here lie in Cave;
If Grave in Cave here buried lie,
Then Grave where is thy Victory?
Go reader, and report, here lies a Cave
Who conquers Death and buries his own Grave.

Here in this grave there lies a Cave,
His father was Knott before him.
He lived Knott, and did Knott die,

Yet underneath this stone does lie;
Knott christened,
Knott begot,
And here he lies,
And yet was Knott.

Here lies a Peck, which some may say
Was first of all a Peck of clay.
This wrought with skill divine while fresh,
Became a curious Peck of flesh.
Through various forms its Maker ran,
Then adding breath, made Peck a man.
Full fifty years Peck felt life's troubles
Till Death relieved a Peck of troubles;
Then fell poor Peck, as all things must,
And here he lies – a Peck of dust.

Husbands have said some harsh things about their late wives; among them was John Dryden, who wrote:

Here lies my wife, here let her lie;
Now she's at rest, and so am I.

But by far the most amusing epitaphs are those that convey an unintentional meaning, or are simply absurd, like these:

Here lie
Father and Mother and Sister and I.
We all died within the space of one short year.
They are all buried at Wimble, except I
and I be buried here.

Here lies the body of John Mound
Lost at sea and never found.

Here lies the body of John Eldred,
At least, he will be when he's dead;
But now at this time he is alive,
The 14th of August, Sixty-five.

Here lies
John Higley
whose father and mother were drowned

in the passage from America.
Had they both lived
they would have been buried here.

> Thos. Woodcock
> Here lie the remains of
> Thomas Woodhen
> The most amiable of husbands
> And excellent of men
> His real name was Woodcock
> But it wouldn't come in rhyme.

Gone to be an angle

Here lies Joseph, Anthony Myonet's son;
Abigail his sister to him is come.
Elemental fire this virgin killed
As she sat on a cock in Stanway's field.

Erected to the memory of
John Philips
accidentally shot
as a mark of affection by his brother.

However, I think that the epitaph that gives me the greatest pleasure and the thought with which I leave you is the simple exclamation on the tombstone of a notorious hypochondriac:

See!

't's leave the last word to my son Piers,
ho wrote this letter to God when he was six:

Dear God
        Thank you for my life.
Will you please help the men tally
handicapped? Please make Spring come sooner
for the winter is biter and and it is
getting cdder and colder and isnt it
too cold? Could you help me with
my maths it is too hard for me? Oh
could you help my brother in South
Africa? Thank you very much for
the birds, the trees, and the louly
scenery, and the elephant and the chinpanzeg
and the parrots, Could you make
everything bright and beautiful

        Lov - frome
            Piers Nimmo

MORE HUMOUR FROM HODDER AND STOUGHTON PAPERBACKS

		CHARLIE ADAMS, GARETH HALE AND NORMAN PACE	
☐	39721 7	Falsies: Forged Diaries of the Famous	£1.95
		SIR LES PATTERSON	
☐	39676 8	The Traveller's Tool	£1.95
		MICHAEL CAINE	
☐	39982 1	And Not Many People Know This Either	£1.95
		WOODY ALLEN	
☐	05235 4	Side Effects	£1.95
		JANET BROWN	
☐	41380 2	Prime Mimicker	£2.50

All these books are available at your local bookshop or newsagent, or can be ordered direct from the publisher. Just tick the titles you want and fill in the form below.

Prices and availability subject to change without notice.

Hodder & Stoughton Paperbacks, P.O. Box 11, Falmouth, Cornwall.

Please send cheque or postal order, and allow the following for postage and packing:

U.K. – 55p for one book, plus 22p for the second book, and 14p for each additional book ordered up to a £1.75 maximum.

B.F.P.O. and EIRE – 55p for the first book, plus 22p for the second book, and 14p per copy for the next 7 books, 8p per book thereafter.

OTHER OVERSEAS CUSTOMERS – £1.00 for the first book, plus 25p per copy for each additional book.

Name ....

Address ....

....